Decorative gardening in containers

Also by Elvin McDonald

A cheese container picked up from a delicatessen forms the frame
for this stylish dining table centerpiece featuring a variegated agave
surrounded by African violets. See Chapter Four.

Decorative gardening in containers

Elvin McDonald

DOUBLEDAY & COMPANY, INC.
GARDEN CITY, NEW YORK
1978

ISBN: 0-385-09590-2
Library of Congress Catalog Card Number 77–92224
Copyright © 1978 by Elvin McDonald

Library of Congress Cataloging in Publication Data

McDonald, Elvin.
  Decorative gardening in containers.

  Bibliography: p. 193.
  1. Container gardening. I. Title.
SB418.M3   635.9′8

To Helen Van Pelt Wilson,
editor, author, friend,
long overdue thanks for keeping
track of the kid from Oklahoma

Contents

       waterproof   148

       Appendixes   179

          Ready-reference lists of plant materials for
             bowl garden landscapes   181
          Plants and supplies by mail   186
          Specialized plant societies and periodicals 190
          Bibliography   193

The making of an author

Helen Van Pelt Wilson, whose name appears on the dedication page of this book, has been challenging and inspiring me since the Christmas of 1948 when, I think it is safe to say, I was the only eleven-year-old boy in the world who both wanted and received a copy of her latest book, *The African Violet*. To me it read like an adventure story, as fascinating as my usual Nancy Drew and Hardy Boys mysteries if not more so.

What I could not have recognized at the time was that this book and its author were to have an enormous influence on my life. Not only did Helen get me to growing African violets successfully, I began to watch for other books and magazine articles bearing her by-line. While she lived in the relatively benign climate of Germantown, Pennsylvania, near Philadelphia, I dared to try anything about which she wrote, even though the weather in western Oklahoma was far less hospitable to plants and gardeners alike.

My first attempt at direct contact with Helen was by telephone in June of 1952. I had just received a letter from my plant pen pal, Peggie Schulz, bearing the news that she had signed a contract with a New York publisher to write a book on gloxinias. Peggie's exuberant letter went on to say that she was sure her editor, Helen Van Pelt Wilson, would be interested in having me do a book also.

Well, to tell the truth, Peggie had already taken my favorite subject. Some two years before, with her help, I had founded the American Gloxinia Society (now called the American Gloxinia and Gesneriad Society) and had begun to publish its bimonthly magazine, *The Gloxinian*. I was listed on the masthead as editor, Peggie as co-editor, and, although she lived in Minneapolis, we managed to communicate surprisingly well by mail.

If Peggie was going to do a book, I wanted to do one. If not gloxinias, how about amaryllis? I grew hundreds of them and even fooled around cross-pollinating and growing new varieties from seed. This suggestion brought a hastily scribbled note from Peggie by return mail: "Hold up on amaryllis; HVPW wants my second book to be about them. I'll help you think of another project."

At first this news depressed me, as I was now running out of my own specialty plants. There were already books about begonias, and HVPW herself had taken geraniums. A correspondent in Austin, Texas, said there was a tremendous need for a book devoted to Chinese hibiscus, but since I didn't have any in my collection, that idea had no immediate appeal.

One day as I was mulling all of this over in my mind, I decided to divide and repot my large *Oxalis crassipes,* one of the few plants in my collection that was rarely without a show of its pink flowers. As my fingers pulled away the old soil, revealing the fleshy rhizomes from which this particular species grows, the thought occurred, why not a book on oxalis? After all, I was growing more than a dozen different kinds, and numerous others were listed in my catalogs from rare-plant specialists.

By the time I had finished potting up all of my *crassipes* divisions, I was convinced that I could do a book devoted entirely to oxalis, and that the idea was too timely to propose by mail. I would telephone Helen Van Pelt Wilson that very afternoon.

When my call to New York finally came through on our party line, I was so excited I could barely talk. "No," I was told, "Mrs. Wilson is not in her office. Would you care to leave a message?"

I was disappointed but undaunted.

"Yes," I said, "I'm calling to propose a book on oxalis."

"On *what?*" The polite voice sounded incredulous.

"OX-uh-liss," I repeated, but still no sound of recognition.

"I'm sorry, you'll have to spell it for me."

"O-x-a-l-i-s." Now I was trying not to reveal my own feelings of incredulity. Didn't everyone know that oxalis was a flowering house plant, not unlike African violets and geraniums?

The voice in New York gave me no encouragement at all. Having gotten my name and address, it ended our conversation with a curt, "I'll have Mrs. Wilson get back to you."

From that moment I tried to stay within earshot of the telephone at all times. I was sure HVPW knew oxalis and would be calling to offer a contract as soon as she received my message.

When, after two or three days, no call came, I began to watch for a letter. Sure enough, before a week had elapsed, I opened up the mailbox one morning and there, right on top, was a squarish note-size envelope bearing a New York City postmark and the engraved name and return address of M. Barrows and Company, Inc., above which had been written in blue fountain-pen ink, "HVPW."

In a flash I tore away the envelope and began to read:

Dear Mr. McDonald:

Thank you for thinking of us for your proposed book on oxalis. However, after much thought we have decided that there is not yet enough interest in this genus to justify publishing a monograph.

However, if you contemplate writing any other gardening books, please keep us in mind.

Very truly yours,

(Mrs.) HELEN VAN PELT WILSON

I was crushed. Instead of a contract, my idol among garden editors and authors had dismissed me with nothing more than a form letter which, I decided, she probably hadn't even signed herself. Clearly, getting into the book-writing business was not as easy as my friend Peggie Schulz had made it seem.

In fact, it was eight years before I received another letter from Helen Van Pelt Wilson and, as fate would have it, the envelope was postmarked June 6, 1960, the day my eldest child, Mark, was born. I was living in New York, attending the Mannes College of Music as a full-time student, majoring in performing opera. In addition I was serving as editor of the eastern edition of *Flower and Garden Magazine* and working two days a week as an editor of outdoor books in the trade department of the Macmillan Company.

Helen's letter was brief and to the point. She was looking for someone to write a definitive book on miniature plants. Would I please call her as soon as possible to arrange a meeting.

My reaction was a mixture of pleasure and doubt. Of course I wanted to do a book, but from my experience at Macmillan, anything labeled "definitive" was far too scholarly to suit me. Nevertheless, I called immediately to set up an appointment. This time the voice at the other end of the line was friendly, cheerful and responsive. It was HVPW herself.

Whatever doubts I may have had about being the author of a "definitive" book on miniature plants, Helen dispelled at our first meeting the next week. "What do you mean, you're not qualified? Look at this file folder—it's filled with tear sheets of feature articles you have been writing about miniature plants."

And so it was. Helen went so far as to say she thought the book was practically half written and, in a matter of minutes, everything was settled. I would submit an outline; the tear sheets of my articles would serve in lieu of the usual sample chapter; a contract was assured, therefore I should start work immediately on the missing parts.

That book was, of course, my first, *Miniature Plants for Home and Greenhouse,* published in 1962 by the D. Van Nostrand Company. Now, from the vantage point of having written some forty books, I have Helen to thank for getting me started. Without her I might never have published a book, a statement numerous author friends of mine could make, notably Charles Marden Fitch, Jacqueline Heriteau and Jack Kramer.

The idea for this book came out of a luncheon Helen and I shared at the Algonquin Hotel in New York on January 30, 1973. Once again she had prepared a folder for me, this time a collection of tear sheets representing my work as the garden editor of *House Beautiful.*

What Helen had perceived was that the craze for terrariums and bottle gardens would soon die down, along with the interest in common foliage plants. To her, the way I had been dressing, grooming, arranging and displaying foliage and flowering house plants in the pages of *HB* suggested a new direction for container gardening.

We parted, having agreed that I would seriously consider the idea. Usually I have to think about these things for at least a few days before an outline begins to take shape, but this time I saw the book in a flash. As I looked around my apartment and my office at *HB,* I realized that Helen's idea really represented the way I was already growing and displaying container plants, yet it was not a practice about which I had consciously written. The next morning I organized and typed my notes and sent the outline off to Helen.

Although I no longer remember the details, there must have been other meetings, because the contract was not drawn until June, by which time my schedule, which had seemed relatively free earlier in the year, was jammed. Even as I signed, I worried that I would not be able to meet the delivery date of January 1, 1974. Considering that it is now January 1978, my worries were not ill-founded.

On the other hand, had my schedule permitted me to meet the original deadline, this book would have been entirely different and not, I suspect, nearly as timely. In fact, it might have been all but forgotten by now. The truth is, the way we perceive gardening and the role plants play in our lives has changed drastically in recent years.

Helen's instincts were right; although we haven't stopped growing terrariums and bottle gardens or nurturing everyday foliage plants, most of us are now looking for new challenges—exotics recently introduced to cultivation, or sophisticated planting and training techniques that we may apply to any plant—rare or common—in order to achieve maximum pleasure from gardening as a way of life.

And, in the final analysis, gardening as a way of life is what this book is about. It represents not only my experiences but those of friends and acquaintances scattered across the length and breadth of this country who have allowed me to photograph their gardens in the years since Helen first proposed the idea of gardening in a bowl to me. My thanks to all, but especially to James McNair, who spent most of one summer creating bowl gardens to set before my camera; Monrovia Nursery for donating the plants James did not have in his own collection; my business partner, Bill Mulligan, for encouragement and constructive criticism all along the way; and Karen Van Westering, my helpful and supportive young editor at Doubleday who must have thought she would be an old woman before I delivered this manuscript.

Elvin McDonald

New York City
January 1978

Introduction

Up until recently most of my writings about plants, in particular the books, have concentrated on how to grow them. Now I would like to explore another facet of gardening, that having to do with the pleasures of combining plants and containers for maximum visual effect. When such a combination is truly successful, the result is a living work of art, one that can be enjoyed briefly in almost any setting and indefinitely in a hospitable environment.

From my viewpoint, all of the gardens included in this book qualify as living works of art, which is to say that each is a visual treat, at least to me. Because they are not natural in such a setting, I have chosen not to include figurines and dollhouse-scale furnishings. True, a ceramic figure may represent a real one, but personally I'd rather use my imagination.

Aesthetics aside, the idea of gardening in a bowl is to take what you have and make it better. There is, for example, nothing wrong with a healthy palm in a big tin can—if it is growing in a nursery or commercial greenhouse. But if it is in your home or office, the simple cosmetic treatment of hiding the can with a basket and carpeting the soil surface with florist sheet moss can do wonders. Or, instead of the moss, try planting a living ground cover such as baby's-tears.

This same idea can be equally effective for a variety of small

Instead of an unruly shrub, pyracantha (firethorn) trained as a bonsai tree stands barely fifteen inches tall. The container is a bonsai tray; the ground cover is a combination of baby's-tears (clipped) and green woods moss. See Chapter Two. Photograph courtesy the Jackson & Perkins Company.

plants growing in utilitarian clay or plastic pots. The cocktail table in my living room is rarely without a bowl or basket filled with flowering and foliage plants taken from my window and fluorescent-light gardens. With moss used to hide the pot rims,

Basic two-step bowl garden: Place waterproof saucer in bottom of basket.

Carpet soil surface with florist sheet moss, sufficient to hide the rim of the pot.

From utilitarian pot to decorative bowl garden in less than two minutes. Created by Bill Mulligan. Photographs by Maddy Miller.

the effect is that of a garden, yet when necessary I can replace one or more pots without disturbing the others.

Right now I have on this table a round wood container which I found on the street in front of a cheese shop. It measures about 22 inches in diameter, 5 inches deep, and holds a half dozen English ivies, a colorfully variegated bromeliad and the wine and silver-green, arrowhead-shaped leaves of an alocasia, all in individual pots even though they appear to grow otherwise.

One of my favorite bowl gardens, which I keep on another table in the living room, has no plants at all. It is filled with potpourri, and each time I sift a few of the petals through my

Instead of plants, potpourri for a bowl garden. The fragrance given off by the petals suggests a garden of roses in full bloom. Photograph by author.

fingers the fragrance they give off makes me think of being in a garden of old-fashioned roses in full bloom.

The bowl garden I enjoy perhaps the most sits on my desk, close enough for me to reach out and touch it as I write. It is a terra-cotta elephant about twelve inches tall, with an opening in the back large enough to accommodate a five-inch plastic pot of *Calathea insignis,* an exotic and colorful foliage plant I find considerably easier to grow than its more common relative, the prayer plant. By day the leaves of the calathea lie mostly in a

A bowl garden that can be eaten—bean sprouts in a hand-thrown clay saucer from the West Indies. See Chapter Three. Created and photographed by James McNair.

horizontal plane, spreading over the elephant as protectively as the branches of a shade tree. At night they fold upward, giving the elephant a splendid if not ridiculous Indian war bonnet.

These examples suggest the endless possibilities for mating plants and containers in combinations or arrangements which I have chosen to call bowl gardens. If gardening in a bowl sounds like another way of saying dish garden, well it could be, but certainly not the mass-produced commercial product that usually consists of several everyday foliage plants jammed together like a bunch of weeds. A wide range of containers and plant materials is available for bowl gardening, both indoors and outdoors, and quite obviously you don't have to have exactly the same container or plants I've used to create similar effects.

Whether you plant your bowl garden in a piece of priceless ex-

Bromeliads such as *Neoregelia Carolinae* tricolor grow well with the roots wrapped in unmilled sphagnum moss and tucked into planting pockets formed in a piece of driftwood. See Chapter Three, especially "Bromeliads on the half shell." Photograph by Hort-Pix.

port china, inexpensive import plastic, or merely a large clay-pot saucer, it can be enormously satisfying. In the final analysis the tactile and totally natural experiences of touching leaves and roots and working the soil with your fingers may be of more importance than the visual rewards of gardening in a bowl.

Decorative gardening in containers

ONE

Bowl gardening basics

For each of the bowl gardens illustrated in Chapters Two, Three, Four, and Five I have included a detailed set of guidelines, a sort of recipe that you can follow to create a similar effect. The basic ingredients are of course the container and the plant—or plants—you choose to place in it, but in the final outcome, success depends on how well you pay attention to details.

And details are what this chapter is about. If I were taking a course in bowl gardening, I would probably want to skip this part and go directly to the planting, which is the way I first used cookbooks. Never mind the dissertations on whisks and baking soda, let me go straight to the stove. Well, some years and a lot of stupid mistakes later, Jean Anderson gave me a copy of *The Doubleday Cookbook,* which she wrote, along with Elaine Hanna. Since Jean is a friend of mine, I decided to read what she had to say up front. Do you know something? It was not only interesting, I found the information enormously helpful.

Now I will be the devil's advocate and say that if I hadn't already put a lot of self-cooked meals on the table and in my stomach, Jean's and Elaine's basics would not have been nearly as meaningful. Therefore, I suggest you read this chapter before you plant your first bowl garden and then come back to it—after a few months or years. You will discover that familiarity with the basics, whether in the kitchen or in the garden, represents a free-

Assorted tropical foliage plants in a growing arrangement. Photograph by author at Longwood Gardens, Kennett Square, Pennsylvania.

dom of expression that comes only when knowledge and experience grow together.

Containers. There is hardly anything that might be called a bowl, dish, pot, pan, basin, vessel, vase, cachepot, jardiniere, tray or planter—made of clay, glass, metal, wood, concrete, plastic, stone or natural fiber—that cannot be used to hold a bowl garden. I draw the line at turning old pianos into planters; otherwise, if the object appeals, try it. I guarantee you'll have fun. All that matters is that your fingers touch nature and your eyes see beauty.

Although the idea of bowl gardening is to plant in containers you have already, for each of those illustrated in this book I have suggested a source. Most are available from local stores, specialty shops, garden centers and nurseries; some are finds from swap meets, garage sales, junk yards and garbage piles; and a few are one-of-a-kind museum-quality pieces.

I have divided the bowl gardens into four chapters, each devoted to containers sharing certain characteristics that affect the way they are used for planting. For example, all of the containers in Chapter Two have drainage holes, those in Chapter Three do not; planting directly in either type is possible but there are definite differences. These are explained in the introductory paragraphs of each chapter.

In Chapter Four the decorative containers used for hiding utilitarian pots may not be waterproof, while those in Chapter Five are. This difference is important for the preservation of the containers as well as the surfaces on which they will rest.

If you are growing a bowl garden comprised entirely of cold-hardy plants, and plan to winter it over outdoors, it may be necessary to take special precautions to protect the container from the potentially harmful effects of alternate freezing and thawing. One way is to remove the garden from its container and bury the rootball in the planting medium of a coldframe. Another is to carry bowl gardens of this type through severely cold weather by keeping them in a sun-heated pit greenhouse—or other glass-enclosed growing space such as a sunroom or regular home greenhouse—that is maintained as cold as possible, but never below about 28° F.

Plants. For each of the bowl gardens included in this book I have specified the plant materials and suggested sources for them. Again, as for the containers, I do not mean to be arbitrary or to imply that bowl gardening requires a big cash investment. The idea is to take what you have and turn it into something better.

On the other hand, I would be the first to admit that I enjoy shopping for plants to fit containers and vice versa. One of the benefits of practicing bowl gardening is that over a period of time you build up a collection of different containers as well as plants. The thing to avoid, of course, is having more bowl gardens at once than you can enjoy. Each requires space in a suitable growing environment and a commitment on your part to attend faithfully its daily needs. What none of us wants is a houseful of dried-up, drowned, overgrown, light-starved or bug-infested bowl gardens.

In order to help you find just the right plant to give the effect you want in a bowl garden I have prepared some ready-reference lists which appear in the Appendix. These are divided according to growth habit into four categories: (1) ground covers, vines and trailers; (2) grass or grasslike; (3) shrub or shrublike; and (4) tree or treelike, with further subdivisions suggesting size. I have also indicated those plants in all categories that are cultivated for flowers in particular.

Special planting techniques. Under this heading for each bowl garden I have explained the steps necessary to prepare and plant the container. I suggest you read the introduction to each chapter, then follow the techniques recommended for the specific bowl garden you are creating.

Before you begin planting, assemble as many tools and supplies as you can foresee needing. Here is a check list to guide your planning:

Tools

Small pruning shears
Manicure scissors
Pocketknife
Garden trowel
Mason's trowel (if you are going to construct a concrete trough
 or sink garden)
Pliers
Soft-bristle brushes (for cleaning leaves and bark)
Mister
Chopsticks (a great help in settling roots and soil in place, espe-
 cially in a small container)
Bonsai pincettes (especially for use in pruning and training
 woody plant materials)
Regular scissors
Single-edged razor blade
Kitchen measuring scoops ($\frac{1}{4}$-, $\frac{1}{3}$-, $\frac{1}{2}$-, 1-cup sizes)
Small hammer
Spoon and fork
Tweezers

Protective linings for containers

Waterproof saucers*
Heavy-duty polyethylene plastic (preferably clear)
Petroleum jelly
Plumber's lead†

* Ordinary unglazed clay-pot saucers are not absolutely waterproof;
glazed ceramic and plastic ones are. To offset the water seepage
through unglazed clay, cut a piece of $\frac{1}{2}$-inch-thick cork to fit under the
saucer; moisture dissipates through the cork.

† Although I have not specified plumber's or flashing lead as a liner for
any of the bowl gardens in this book, it is an excellent material to have
on hand. Rolls 12 or 14 inches wide are available from plumbing supply

Growing mediums

Potting soil
Sphagnum peat moss
Vermiculite
Builder's (or "clean, sharp") sand
Well-rotted compost
Charcoal chips
Sphagnum moss (unmilled)
Perlite
Leafmold
Clay subsoil
Blocks of osmunda fiber (for use in building up multilevel plant-
   ings)

Mulches/ground covers

Florist sheet moss
Pebbles
Stones
Bark chips
Green woods moss‡
Gravel
Marble chips
Small seashells

---

houses. Plumber's lead is easily cut with tin shears, the edges then bent up to form the walls. Unless you purposely punch a drainage hole in the bottom, the container will be waterproof.

‡ If your garden supports a healthy stand of green woods moss, simply take a putty knife and lift enough pieces to lay the size carpet you have in mind. If not, ask permission to gather some from another's property, then grow your own crop. Here's how:

   1. Gather moss with about a half inch of soil.

Miscellaneous supplies

Copper wire (medium gauge)
Pieces of driftwood
Galvanized screen wire to cover drainage holes
Interesting rocks
Masking tape
Epoxy glue
Plant ties
Florist wire and tape

Owner/owners. Let's face it, every plant and bowl garden I own is not as picture perfect as the ones I have chosen to show in this book. That's why I've included the names of the owners along with the descriptions.

The three whose handiwork appears most, Ernesta and Fred Ballard and James McNair, live on opposite sides of the continent—the Ballards in Philadelphia, James in San Francisco—yet during the same time period I found all of them involved in a similar pursuit of horticultural and artistic excellence. Seeing and photographing their collections has in particular influenced not

---

2. Place in a tray to dry, then crumble away most of the soil, saving the dried-up green parts.

3. Make a mixture of equal parts all-purpose potting soil and sphagnum peat moss; spread a half inch deep in a shallow glass baking dish or aluminum foil tray.

4. Cover the soil-peat with a single layer of cheesecloth; sprinkle the dried-up moss on the surface; cover with another layer of cheesecloth.

5. Mist until well moistened.

6. Place to sprout in bright light but no direct sun, where temperatures range between 70° F. and 80° F.

7. Check daily to be sure the cheesecloth is moist; if not, mist as necessary. Within eight weeks you should see promising green and in another month your moss carpet will be ready to lay.

only the content of this book, but the way I personally grow, enjoy and display my plants.

Environment. Some of the bowl gardens in this book are meant to be used only briefly, as bouquets of cut flowers, then returned to optimum growing conditions. Most, however, are intended to suggest permanent gardens that can be cultivated indefinitely. Therefore, I have outlined the suggested care and treatment of each, as follows:

Light. "Bright" suggests natural light strong enough to read by, but little or no direct sun. "Up to a half day of sun" might be in or near an exposure facing east, south or west that affords a few hours of direct sun. "Half day or more of sun" means exactly what it says, most often found indoors in unobstructed windows facing southeast, south or southwest.

Rock-planted *Ficus diversifolia* bonsai, with *Ficus pumila* ground cover, grows in a sunny window garden belonging to Ernesta and Fred Ballard.

Subtropical shrub and tree seedlings, in the early stages of bonsai training, grow in author's fluorescent-light garden.

The phrase "fluorescent-light garden" suggests the placement of two or more fluorescent tubes directly over a shelf or table of plants. The best tubes for growing plants are those in 20-, 30-, 40- and 72-watt sizes, which come, respectively, in lengths of 24, 36, 48 and 96 inches. Combine one Cool White and one Warm White tube in each fixture, or use special plant-growth tubes. Plug the lights into a timer in order to assure days and nights of uniform length. In cooler temperatures I find that twelve-hour daily periods of light are sufficient for most plants, but in the warmth of the average dwelling or office, fourteen to sixteen are better.

Some bowl gardens may be grown within the brightest circle of light produced by an ordinary incandescent bulb in a table lamp that is burned fourteen to sixteen hours daily. This is also an excellent way to supplement natural light when you know it isn't bright enough to sustain optimum growth, especially if the lamp is one you would burn anyway for general room illumination.

It is also possible to use special incandescent plant floodlights to nurture bowl gardens and show them off at night. These are available generally in a range of 75 to 150 watts in the form of reflector floods. I recommend that these be used only in ceramic or porcelain sockets. Since floodlights give off considerable heat, be careful not to place one so close to a plant that the leaves will be burned. The heat also tends to dry out the atmosphere, which means you may have to water the roots and mist the leaves more frequently.

TEMPERATURE. I have included bowl gardens in this book that can be kept cold (usually not below 28° F.) or cool (40–55° F.) in fall and winter, as well as those that need moderate (55–70° F.) or warm (65–80° F.) temperatures. In warm, frost-free weather most will grow well in the average dwelling or office, or outdoors (but only if the container has drainage holes so that rainwater can escape).

If you like the appearance of a certain bowl garden, but the plants used in it require cooler or warmer temperatures than you can provide, simply substitute lookalikes better suited to your environment. (Check the ready-reference lists in the Appendix.)

HUMIDITY. Although cacti and other succulents from the desert will do well indoors in an atmosphere that is dry, most plants (as well as people) will be healthier if the surrounding air contains a range of 40 to 60 per cent relative humidity, which I specify as "medium." "High" suggests a moisture-laden atmosphere that rarely can be maintained outside a humidified plant room or greenhouse.

To maintain a medium amount of humidity in my apartment during the heating season I use cool-vapor humidifiers and pebble trays kept nearly filled with water. I do a lot of misting, which I find doesn't do much in the way of increasing the percentage of relative humidity, but it keeps my bowl gardens and other plants rain-fresh and is good therapy for me.

In connection with humidity, you will notice that I frequently recommend fresh-air circulation. I hope you live where there is fresher air than we have in New York, but even here I consider it essential to keep a window open slightly in each room where I grow plants (which is all of them). The only time I don't is during periods of extreme temperatures outdoors, either hot or cold, when I don't want to overtax the air-conditioning and heating units. One reason I prescribe fresh-air circulation for most plants is that it is an excellent natural deterrent to red spider mites.

SOIL MIXES. For each bowl garden I have recommended a suitable growing medium. Unless you have your own special mixes, I suggest these basic recipes:

All-purpose. Combine three parts packaged all-purpose potting soil or well-rotted compost with two parts sphagnum peat moss (put through a quarter-inch screen to remove twigs and other debris) and one part coarse builder's sand or perlite. If you have no compost and the packaged potting soil seems too heavy and dense, add one part horticultural vermiculite.

Cactus/succulent. Mix together three parts coarse builder's sand to two parts sphagnum peat moss and one part soil or compost. To each quart of these combined ingredients add one tablespoon of dolomitic limestone or steamed bone meal.

Alpine. Combine equal parts packaged all-purpose potting soil, well-rotted leaf mold, sphagnum peat moss and clean, sharp sand. To each quart (or five-inch pot) of these ingredients combined, add one tablespoon of dolomitic limestone (unless you know the alpine you are about to plant needs a growing medium on the acid side of the soil pH scale, that is, below 7.0).

SOIL MOISTURE. In my experience, most plants cultivated in containers do well in soil that is kept evenly moist to slightly on the dry side, which is to say neither sopping wet nor bone dry. Cyperus and aglaonema (Chinese evergreen) will live standing in water, but it is hard to think of other plants that will tolerate either extreme for long; even cacti and other succulents from the desert will soon wither in a growing medium that is bone dry.

Deciding how much and when to water a bowl garden depends mostly on common sense. If you wait until the leaves have wilted visibly, you've waited too long. Since the actual growing medium used in most bowl gardens is hidden by a mulch or ground cover of moss, pebbles, sand or gravel, the thing to do is reach a finger underneath and poke around. If it feels wet, don't water; in fact, if the container has no drainage holes, maybe you need to tip it to one side and wait to see if any excess moisture will drain out. If the growing medium feels pleasantly moist or damp, wait to add water for a day or two. But if a pinch of the surface soil feels dry, it is probably time to water.

If you have used fresh florist sheet moss or green woods moss as the ground cover, watch for slight dulling in its color, often a sign that the time to water is drawing near. However, if the soil underneath feels moist, all you need to do is give the moss a good misting.

If your bowl garden is in a relatively deep container without drainage holes, a vase for example, I recommend using a soil moisture meter, at least until a watering routine is established. By inserting the meter probe deep into the soil, you can determine almost precisely the availability of moisture where the roots are. Sometimes the surface soil feels dry even though the deepest roots may be standing in water.

How you water the growing medium of a bowl garden depends on its size as well as the type of container. For anything that might be considered a miniature landscape I moisten the soil by using a bulb baster from the kitchen. For larger plantings I use my trusty watering can. Outdoors the handiest way to water is with a hose turned to a gentle stream.

Bowl gardens without drainage holes require certain restraint at watering time, otherwise excess moisture may accumulate around the roots and cause them to rot. For this reason I recommend placing only containers with drainage holes outdoors, unless they can be shielded from rains.

If too much water gathers in the bottom of a decorative container that serves only to hide a utilitarian pot, it's a relatively simple matter to pour off the excess, but if you have planted directly in a drainless container, there is no easy solution. In this situation James McNair suggests inserting a piece of plastic tubing all the way to the bottom and suctioning off as much of the excess as possible.

FERTILIZER. For each of the bowl gardens included in this book I have indicated when and when not to make light applications of fertilizer. By "light" I mean to suggest mixing the fertilizer at about half the strength recommended on the label for potted plants. I find it generally best not to apply fertilizer from about Labor Day to St. Valentine's, except in a fluorescent-light garden where growing conditions usually remain essentially the same all year.

TWO

Gardening in a bowl
with drainage holes

The containers used for the bowl gardens in this chapter have one important thing in common with ordinary clay and plastic flowerpots: all have drainage holes to permit the rapid runoff of excess moisture.

From a cultural viewpoint, this means that they are more easily handled by the busy person who often has to water in a hurry, or by the gardener who tends to overwater. In addition, bowl gardens with drainage holes adapt readily to an indoor/outdoor existence—meaning they can be kept indoors in fall and winter, outdoors (if possible) during frost-free weather in spring and summer.

Since the containers illustrated in this chapter all have drainage holes, presumably they were intended for planting and therefore require no special handling to protect the interior from moisture or scratches. Establishing plants in them requires essentially the same procedures one uses in planting standard clay or plastic pots, with one exception: most are broad and shallow instead of narrow and deep, which means that they will require more frequent watering in order to maintain an optimum level of moisture in the growing medium.

Flowering alpine perennials grow in a clay bulb pan twelve inches in diameter and six inches deep. Photograph by Ralph Bailey.

1   Cacti and other succulents

CONTAINERS: Glazed ceramic bonsai pots (foreground) and unglazed, plain clay pots, without thickened rims (background), probably from Europe. *Sources:* Bonsai specialists, plant shops, nurseries (see Appendix).

PLANTS: Two species of *Sedum* (foreground), a *Mammillaria* cactus (background left) and an *Echeveria* (background right). *Sources:* Plant shops, specialists in cacti and other succulents (see Appendix).

SPECIAL PLANTING TECHNIQUE: None required.

OWNERS: Ernesta and Fred Ballard.

Cacti and other succulents.

ENVIRONMENT:

Light: Sun at least four hours daily, or grow six inches directly beneath the tubes in a fluorescent-light garden.

Temperature: Cool to moderate in winter (40–70° F.), average dwelling or office in other seasons, or outdoors in frost-free weather.

Humidity: Low to medium; fresh-air circulation is important.

Soil Mix: Cactus/succulent (see Chapter One).

Soil Moisture: Evenly moist to slightly on the dry side in spring and summer; on the dry side in fall and winter.

Fertilizer: Make light applications in spring and summer only.

COMMENTS: Keep withering or dead leaves picked off. Replace old soil with fresh in late winter or early spring; if sedums have any long, unruly stems, especially those not fully clothed with leaves, cut back to the base of the plant to encourage and make room for new growth.

2   Alpine asperula

CONTAINER: Unglazed terra-cotta pot with fluted rim, from Italy. *Sources:* Plant shops, nurseries, specialists in garden statuary (see Appendix).

PLANT: *Asperula nitida puberla,* a herbaceous alpine perennial, related to the more common *A. odorata* (sweet woodruff of herb gardens). *Sources:* Specialists in alpine plants (see Appendix).

SPECIAL PLANTING TECHNIQUE: Inch-deep mulch of shale; rock chips keep excess moisture from standing in the crown of the plant and also serve to show it off.

Alpine asperula.

OWNERS: Ernesta and Fred Ballard.

ENVIRONMENT:

Light: Full sun in spring, part shade in summer.

Temperature: Cold to cool in fall and winter (28–50° F.), moderate (55–75° F.) in spring and summer. In climates where summer typically brings hot, muggy weather, situate an alpine planting like this where there is protection from direct sun during the hottest part of the day.

Humidity: Medium, but always in the presence of fresh air that circulates freely.

Soil Mix: Alpine (see Chapter One).

Soil Moisture: Evenly moist to slightly on the dry side in spring and summer; on the dry side in fall and winter.

Fertilizer: Make light applications in spring and summer only.

COMMENTS: Container culture of alpine plants assures giving them the rapid drainage of excess moisture they need, and also permits moving to the best possible environment with each seasonal change in the weather. Replace old soil with fresh every two or three years, in late winter or early spring. Do not attempt alpines as container plants unless you have a protected, nearly freezing place to keep them in winter, such as a cold frame, pit greenhouse or greenhouse maintained at just above 32° F.

3   Sedum in strawberry jar

CONTAINER: Unglazed clay strawberry jar. *Sources:* Plant shops, nurseries (see Appendix).

PLANT: *Sedum spathulifolium* 'Capa Blanca.' *Sources:* Nurseries, specialists in cacti and other succulents (see Appendix).

SPECIAL PLANTING TECHNIQUE: Place layer of drainage in bottom of jar; add potting mix to level of planting pockets; position one or more plants in each and spread out the roots inside; continue adding potting mix to fill the jar, then plant one or more sedums in the top opening; add pebble mulch.

OWNERS: Ernesta and Fred Ballard.

ENVIRONMENT:

Light: Sun at least four hours daily.

Temperature: Cold to cool in fall and winter (28–50° F.), average dwelling, office or garden in other seasons.

Humidity: Low to medium, with fresh air.

Soil Mix: Cactus/succulent (see Chapter One).

Soil Moisture: Evenly moist to slightly on the dry side in spring and summer; on the dry side in fall and winter.

Fertilizer: Make light applications in spring and summer only.

COMMENTS: Some sedums can withstand frost, others cannot; this one can, but as a container plant it is best wintered in a coldframe, pit greenhouse or other protected place.

Sedum in strawberry jar.

4   Sempervivum in bonsai tray

CONTAINER: Glazed clay bonsai tray, available in various earth and sky colors. *Sources:* Bonsai specialists, plant shops, nurseries (see Appendix).

PLANTS: One common species of *Sempervivum* or hen-and-chickens, a succulent that grows with abandon in countless gardens. *Sources:* Your own garden or that of a friend, nurseries, specialists in cacti and other succulents (see Appendix).

SPECIAL PLANTING TECHNIQUE: None required.

OWNERS: Ernesta and Fred Ballard.

ENVIRONMENT:

Light: Sun at least four hours daily, or grow four inches directly beneath the tubes in a fluorescent-light garden.

Temperature: Cold to cool in fall and winter (28–50° F.), average dwelling, office or garden in other seasons.

Humidity: Low to medium, but always needs fresh air.

Soil Mix: Cactus/succulent (see Chapter One).

Soil Moisture: Evenly moist to slightly on the dry side in spring and summer; on the dry side in fall and winter.

Fertilizer: Make light applications in spring and summer.

COMMENTS: Most sempervivums can withstand frost, but as container plants they are best wintered in a coldframe, pit greenhouse or other protected place. Remove some old soil and replace with fresh every two or three years, in late winter or early spring; replant, using mostly the younger, small- to medium-size leaf rosettes.

Sempervivum in bonsai tray.

5   **Sempervivums in bonsai tray**

CONTAINER: Glazed clay bonsai tray, available in various earth
and sky colors; this one is dark blue and measures slightly less
than 1 inch deep. *Sources:* Bonsai specialists, plant shops,
nurseries (see Appendix).

PLANTS: *Sempervivum arachnoideum,* one of the hen-and-
chickens, or cobweb houseleeks, so-called because of white,
weblike threads that crisscross each plant from leaf to leaf.
Sources: Your own garden or that of a friend, nurseries, specialists in cacti and other succulents (see Appendix).

SPECIAL PLANTING TECHNIQUE: Cover drainage holes with inch

Sempervivums in bonsai tray.

squares of galvanized screen wire held in place with a piece or two of masking tape. Add a scant layer of coarse sand or chicken grit, then fill with enough potting soil to form a mound equal to one or one and a half times the height of the tray. Plant one or more sempervivums on the mound, then carpet any bare soil with moss and a few pebbles.

OWNERS: Ernesta and Fred Ballard.

ENVIRONMENT:

Light: Sun at least four hours daily, or grow four inches directly beneath the tubes in a fluorescent-light garden.

Temperature: Cold to cool in fall and winter (28–50° F.), average dwelling, office or garden in other seasons.

Humidity: Low to medium, but always needs fresh air.

Soil Mix: Cactus/succulent (see Chapter One).

Soil Moisture: Evenly moist to slightly on the dry side in spring and summer; on the dry side in fall and winter.

Fertilizer: Make light applications in spring and summer only.

COMMENTS: Most sempervivums can withstand frost, but as container plants they are best wintered in a coldframe, pit greenhouse or other protected place. Replace old soil with fresh every two or three years, in late winter or early spring; replant, using mostly the younger, small- to medium-size leaf rosettes.

6   Living stones in bonsai tray

CONTAINER: Glazed bonsai tray measuring approximately 5 by 8 inches and 2 inches deep; available in various earth and sky colors. *Sources:* Bonsai specialists, plant shops, nurseries (see Appendix).

PLANTS: Three species of *Lithops,* commonly called living stones because of their uncanny resemblance to the stones among which they grow wild in South Africa. *Sources:* Plant shops, specialists in cacti and other succulents (see Appendix).

SPECIAL PLANTING TECHNIQUE: Cover drainage holes with inch squares of galvanized screen wire held in place with masking tape. Add a scant layer of gravel, then fill to a half inch below the rim with potting soil. Position rocks and plant lithops, taking care to position them at the same level in the soil as they were in their original containers. Mulch all around with pebbles, gravel or stone chips.

OWNER: Grigsby Cactus Gardens.

ENVIRONMENT:

Light: Sun at least four hours daily, or grow four inches below the tubes in a fluorescent-light garden.

Temperature: Cool to moderate in fall and winter (40–70° F.), average dwelling, office or garden in spring and summer.

Humidity: Low to medium, but always needs fresh air.

Soil Mix: Cactus/succulent (see Chapter One).

Soil Moisture: Evenly moist to slightly on the dry side in spring and summer; on the dry side in fall and winter.

Fertilizer: Make light applications in spring and summer only.

COMMENTS: Be very careful about overwatering lithops during periods of hot, humid weather. A planting like this one should not require repotting for at least two to three years. Remove old leaves as they shrivel and die to make room for new growth.

Living stones in bonsai tray.

7   Olive tree bonsai

CONTAINER: Glazed bonsai tray approximately 9 by 15 inches and 1 inch deep. *Sources:* Bonsai specialists, plant shops, nurseries (see Appendix).

PLANTS: Common olive (*Olea europaea*) with two kinds of moss. *Sources:* Olive from nurseries (see Appendix); moss from garden or woods (for how to grow your own supply of moss, see Chapter One).

SPECIAL PLANTING TECHNIQUE: This bowl garden represents bonsai at its finest, an art form comprised of enough specialized and variable techniques to fill a lifetime of learning. However, I have chosen to include it in this book for two reasons:

1. The olive is subtropical in nature and therefore more easily managed as a container plant in North America than the temperate-climate trees and shrubs of traditional bonsai. (For a complete list of tropical and subtropical woody plants suited to this kind of training, see Appendix.)

2. Establishing the roots of a plant on a piece of rock and then gradually exposing certain of them in the most artistic and natural manner possible is a bonsai technique that is equally useful in bowl gardening. Here's how:

Look for flat-bottomed rocks with an interesting surface, ideally with a few nooks and crannies to hold some growing medium. If, by chance, you find your rock along the seashore, soak it in fresh water for several months, then proceed with planting.

Although it is possible to find rocks shaped in such a way that no other container need be provided to hold growing medium for the roots, I suggest you first try by situating the rock in a shallow bonsai tray of soil (as shown in the photograph on page 29).

In the general area of the rock where you want to establish a woody plant, use epoxy cement to attach four or five pieces

Olive tree bonsai.

of ✗21 copper wire, each two or three inches long and bent into a U or hairpin shape. (Apply adhesive at the bend in the wire.) These will serve to hold the plant in place until the roots take hold on the rock's surface.

The next step is to bare the roots of the tree or shrub you have selected. This represents a considerable shock, so fall or winter are usually the best times since the plant will likely be in a state of semirest. Crumble away as much of the soil as you can with your fingers, then finish by washing the roots under a gentle stream of water.

Untangle and spread the roots out over the rock, spacing at least three of the largest more or less equidistant from each other to assure a firm hold. Lightly tie the copper wires around the main roots to hold everything in place while you proceed. Make up a paste consisting of clay subsoil (from your own garden, that of a friend, from bonsai specialists), sphagnum peat moss and water; smear this along the surface of the rock where you want to attach roots, press the roots in place and cover with more of the paste. Now you can tighten the wire twists, first stuffing little wads of sphagnum moss between the wires and those points along the roots where they will be tied.

The next step is to bring the rest of the roots down around the rock and, if long enough, into the soil of the container in which it is placed. Paint any roots that remain exposed with the clay subsoil and peat moss glue. Finally, cover all of the roots on the rock with green woods moss.

If all goes well, you can begin to expose some of the roots after about eight months. Start at the trunk and work gradually, using your fingers to expose a little more of the roots perhaps every six to eight weeks. You can trim off small roots, but keep the big ones. Be especially careful not to remove or expose a large number of the white-tipped feeder roots at any given time.

Success with a planting of this type depends largely on never, repeat never, allowing it to dry out. In hot weather thorough watering may be needed twice a day. Even while you are in the process of planting, it may be necessary to mist the exposed roots from time to time.

To learn the basic techniques for training bonsai, take a course or, if that is not possible, study some books on the subject (see also Appendix for specific suggestions for reading matter related to gardening in a bowl).

OWNERS: Ernesta and Fred Ballard.

ENVIRONMENT:

> *Light:* Sunny window indoors, partial shade outdoors; responds to fluorescent-light culture in cold weather if summered outdoors.
>
> *Temperature:* Cool to moderate in fall and winter (28–65° F.), average dwelling, office or garden in spring and summer.
>
> *Humidity:* Medium to high, but always needs fresh air.
>
> *Soil Mix:* All-purpose (see Chapter One).
>
> *Soil Moisture:* Evenly moist at all times.
>
> *Fertilizer:* Make light applications in spring and summer only.

COMMENTS: Replace most of the old soil with fresh every year or two, ideally in late winter or early spring. At the same time it will be necessary to thin and prune back the roots that have been growing in the soil, but usually not more than you remove of the top parts—leaves, twigs, branches—in the same operation. In other words, if you remove approximately a fourth of the root system, then you should remove approximately a fourth of the top parts.

8   Natural rock planter

CONTAINER: Nearly flat-bottomed piece of rock found in nature with slightly concave surface and crevices to hold roots and soil. *Sources:* If you can't find a suitable rock in nature, purchase some Featherock from a plant shop or nursery (or check your Yellow Pages under "Stone—Natural" for a local dealer). Featherock is a naturally lightweight volcanic stone in which you can hollow planting pockets fairly easily using a hammer and cold chisel.

PLANTS: The miniature tree is 'Kingsville' boxwood (*Buxus*) with a ground cover of baby's-tears; the foreground plants, left to right, are sweet-alyssum (in bloom), *Equisetum scirpoides* and *Acorus gramineus pusillus*. *Sources:* Plant shops, nurseries, specialists in rare plants (see Appendix).

SPECIAL PLANTING TECHNIQUE: Establish the tree on the stone according to the guidelines given for the olive tree bonsai (photograph on page 29). Fill crevices and pockets in the stone with soil and set other plants into these. Cover any exposed soil with green woods moss or small pebbles. Keep in the shade and mist heavily two or three times a day until the plants are established.

OWNERS: Ernesta and Fred Ballard.

ENVIRONMENT:

Light: Sunny window indoors, partial shade outdoors; responds to fluorescent-light culture in cold weather if summered outdoors.

Temperature: Cool to moderate in fall and winter (28–65° F.), average dwelling, office or garden in spring and summer.

Humidity: Medium to high, but always needs fresh air.

Soil Mix: All-purpose (see Chapter One).

Soil Moisture: Evenly moist at all times, which means you may have to soak it twice a day in hot weather.

Natural rock planter.

Fertilizer: Make light applications in spring and summer only.

COMMENTS: Sweet-alyssum is an annual; replace each spring with one or two seedlings. Temperatures below 28° F. may kill the baby's-tears, but it can be quickly re-established in the spring. If given good care a rock planting like this one can be kept going for many years simply by replacing a little of the old soil with fresh in late winter or early spring. In really cold weather I suggest keeping it in a coldframe or pit greenhouse.

9   Concrete sink or trough garden

CONTAINER: Concrete, approximately 10 by 20 inches by 5 inches deep. *Sources:* Rarely available outside of England, but you can cast your own. Here's how:

Use a fairly good grade of lumber to make the forms; the measurements given here are for a container the size of the one shown; for other dimensions, adjust accordingly, allowing for walls approximately 1 inch thick.

For the outside form you will need two 1 by 5s 10 inches long and two 1 by 5s 20 inches long; screw together and tack in place with nails on a piece of thick plywood. Nail one or two medium-size corks (at least 1½ inches long) in the plywood wherever you would like drainage holes.

Mix concrete (I use bagged mix sold for patching sidewalks) and pour inside the form; level off to a fairly uniform depth of 1 inch, sloping the inside just slightly toward the corks.

Now insert the inside form, for which you will need two 1 by 4s 8 inches long and two 1 by 4s 18 inches long. For ease in removing these after they have served their purpose, I secure them to the outside form with short battens (pieces of 1 by 2 scrap lumber about 4 inches long); nail the battens to the inside form, then set it in place on the newly poured concrete bottom and tack battens to top of outside form.

Fill the sides with concrete and smooth off at the top, even with the forms.

Allow concrete to set overnight (12–18 hours), then remove forms, but carefully. Now is the time, before the concrete is hard set, to round off edges and corners with a putty knife or mason's trowel. If you would like the exterior walls and edges to have a rough, weathered appearance, run a wire brush over them.

Leave to dry for another twelve to eighteen hours, but spray lightly with water every three or four hours to keep the concrete from developing cracks. After this time the container is ready to be cured by soaking in a dark pink solution of potassium permanganate (your pharmacist should be able to get it for you) for a few days. (This is to neutralize the concrete's acidity.) After this treatment, allow to dry for a week or two, then proceed with planting.

PLANTS: Clockwise, beginning top center, dwarf nandina, *Andromeda polifolia nana,* drabis (rock-cress), *Viola macedonica, Thymus minus, Draba sibirica, Sedum dasyphyllum* and *Damnacanthus italica. Sources:* Nurseries and specialists in rare plants (see Appendix).

Concrete sink or trough garden.

This concrete planter is perhaps twice the size of the one described previously; note the thicker walls. Here it serves as a home for assorted alpines and dwarf evergreens, all seeming to grow out of natural stone outcroppings. Because of its weight this planter enjoys a permanent position in a fairly protected part of the Philadelphia garden of Ernesta and Fred Ballard.

SPECIAL PLANTING TECHNIQUE: Add layer of pebbles or pot shards for drainage, then position rocks, add soil and proceed with planting. Cover bare spots with green woods moss.

OWNERS: Ernesta and Fred Ballard.

ENVIRONMENT:

Light: Sunny window indoors, partial shade outdoors; responds to fluorescent-light culture in cold weather if summered outdoors.

Temperature: Cool to moderate in fall and winter (28–65° F.), outdoors in spring and summer.

Humidity: Medium to high, but always needs fresh air.

Soil Mix: All-purpose (see Chapter One) or alpine.

Soil Moisture: Evenly moist at all times.

Fertilizer: Make light applications in spring and summer only.

COMMENTS: Although the plants in this particular garden can withstand considerable cold and in fact need at least six to eight weeks of near freezing temperatures in fall and early winter to initiate dormancy, innumerable miniature or dwarf tropicals or subtropicals might be used to create a similar effect in a concrete container destined for window or light garden that is warm (60–75° F.) all year; for lists, see Appendix.

A coldframe, pit greenhouse or plant room kept barely above freezing in fall and winter would be an excellent place to keep a sink garden planted with hardy perennials and alpines as the one in the photograph is.

10   Polyscias bonsai

CONTAINER: Glazed ceramic bonsai tray. *Source:* Bonsai specialists, plant shops, nurseries (see Appendix).

PLANT: *Polyscias fruticosa,* the so-called ming aralia. *Source:* Plant shops, nurseries (see Appendix).

SPECIAL PLANTING TECHNIQUE: Polyscias often reacts adversely to root disturbance or a change in environment. When transplanting from a standard pot to a bonsai tray, it will help the plant adjust if you enclose the entire planting in a plastic bag for a week or two; during this time keep in bright light but little or no direct sun, or place in a fluorescent-light garden.

OWNER: Paul Galka.

ENVIRONMENT:

Light: Half day of sun, or grow in a fluorescent-light garden. Outdoors in frost-free weather polyscias will do well in partial shade.

Temperature: Moderate in winter (55–70° F.), average dwelling or office in other seasons, or outdoors in frost-free weather.

Humidity: Medium to high, but with fresh-air circulation.

Soil Mix: All-purpose (see Chapter One).

Soil Moisture: Evenly moist to slightly on the dry side; excessive wetness or dryness will cause rapid defoliation.

Fertilizer: Make light applications all year.

COMMENTS: This polyscias just naturally gives the effect of an aged bonsai at all stages of growth—from rooted cuttings a few inches tall to ceiling-high specimens that command prices in the vicinity of $500—which is why it is commonly called the ming aralia.

Polyscias bonsai.

11   Geranium bonsai

CONTAINER: Glazed ceramic bonsai pot (five-inch diameter). *Source:* Bonsai specialists, plant shops, nurseries (see Appendix).

PLANT: Dwarf geranium. *Sources:* Local plant shops or by mail from specialists (see Appendix).

SPECIAL PLANTING TECHNIQUE: None required.

OWNER: Zelma Clark.

ENVIRONMENT:

Light: Half day or more of direct sun, or grow four inches directly beneath the tubes in a fluorescent-light garden.

Temperature: Moderate in winter (55–70° F.), average dwelling or office in other seasons, or outdoors in frost-free weather.

Humidity: Low to medium; fresh-air circulation is vital.

Soil Mix: All-purpose (see Chapter One).

Soil Moisture: Evenly moist to slightly on the dry side.

Fertilizer: Make light applications of a flowering-type fertilizer all year.

COMMENTS: Miniature and dwarf geraniums are among the easiest of all plants to prune and train for an almost instant effect of aged bonsai. By practicing the standard bonsai techniques of root and top pruning at repotting time, it is possible to keep the plant in the same pot almost indefinitely. Small-leaved scented geraniums such as lemon (*Pelargonium crispum*) and apple (*P. odoratissimum*) also respond well to bonsai treatment.

Geranium bonsai.

12   Blue Delftware planter

CONTAINER: Blue Delftware planter with porcelain liner. *Source:* Tiffany (see Appendix).

PLANTS: Mimosa tree with selaginella ground cover. *Sources:* Mimosa from Monrovia Nursery (wholesale only); available from local plant shops, nurseries or by mail from specialists (see Appendix); selaginella from plant shops or mail-order specialists (see Appendix).

SPECIAL PLANTING TECHNIQUE: None required.

OWNER: James McNair.

ENVIRONMENT:

Light: Sun at least four hours daily; may be wintered in a fluorescent-light garden.

Temperature: Cool to moderate in winter (40–70° F.), average dwelling or office in other seasons, or outdoors in frost-free weather.

Humidity: Medium to high; fresh-air circulation is important.

Soil Mix: All-purpose (see Chapter One).

Soil Moisture: Evenly moist at all times.

Fertilizer: Make light applications in spring and summer only.

COMMENTS: The same or similar effect may be achieved by combining any of the ground covers with the shrubs and trees listed in the Appendix of this book.

Blue Delftware planter.

13   Begonia bonsai

CONTAINER: Glazed ceramic bonsai tray with matching saucer. *Source:* Bonsai specialists, plant shops, nurseries (see Appendix).

PLANT: Begonia 'Tor Two,' a semituberous cultivar with miniature begonia used as ground cover. *Sources:* Specialists in begonias and other rare plants (see Appendix).

SPECIAL PLANTING TECHNIQUE: None required.

OWNER: Jack Golding.

ENVIRONMENT:

Light: Half day of sun, or grow in a fluorescent-light garden.

Temperature: Moderate in winter (55–70° F.), average dwelling or office in other seasons, or outdoors in frost-free weather.

Humidity: Medium to high; fresh-air circulation is important.

Soil Mix: All-purpose (see Chapter One) or use owner Golding's, which is three parts vermiculite, three parts sphagnum peat moss and four parts perlite, plus one level tablespoon of ground limestone to every eight quarts of the mix.

Soil Moisture: Evenly moist to slightly on the dry side.

Fertilizer: Make light applications in spring and summer, little or none in fall and winter.

COMMENTS: There are numerous small-leaved, upright begonias that may be pruned and trained to give the effect of a bonsai and since, by nature, begonias tend to be shallow-rooted, they respond well to culture in trays only two or three inches deep.

Begonia bonsai.

THREE

Gardening in a bowl without drainage holes

The containers used for the bowl gardens in this chapter are all waterproof. In fact, a number of them suggest water as the growing medium instead of soil. They range in size from miniatures you can cup in one hand to a half-barrel water-lily garden that weighs several hundred pounds.

Once you learn the simple technique of planting in a drainless container, endless possibilities will come to mind. Actually, the planting isn't tricky at all, but deciding when and how much to water can be. Since there is no way for excess moisture to escape, the danger lies in adding too much water at once which can lead to foul-smelling soil and rotted roots. For this reason I do not recommend placing drainless bowl gardens outdoors, since one heavy rain is all it takes to drown them. For specific instructions and suggestions about watering, please refer to the main discussion on this subject in Chapter One.

The general rule I follow in planting a container that has no drainage holes is to begin with a layer of gravel or pebbles equal to a third or fourth of its height, topped by a sprinkling of charcoal chips. Then I add some soil and continue in more or less the same way I would with an ordinary clay or plastic flowerpot. "Geraniums in crystal cylinder" on page 51 clearly shows what I am talking about.

Cacti and other succulents grow in a desertscape planted in a glazed ceramic casserole. Created by Bill Mulligan.

The purpose of this extra-thick layer of drainage materials is to permit air to reach the roots. In case of overwatering the excess will evaporate more quickly from pebbles or gravel than from potting soil, and the charcoal chips help to keep everything in the container—soil, roots, water—in a fresh, healthy state.

Since containers without drainage holes are usually intended for some purpose other than holding soil and the roots of a plant, it may be necessary to take certain precautionary measures before planting in them. One solution for good bowls (china, silver, other precious metals) is to have a galvanized metal liner made to exact dimensions, or to find an inexpensive plastic liner that fits. The outer edges can be camouflaged with ground cover plants (baby's-tears, for example) or florist sheet moss.

Obviously, having a liner custom made is relatively expensive, that is if you can find someone to fabricate it in the first place, and finding exactly the right size plastic container may be impossible. Therefore, I suggest an alternative which I learned several years ago from my gardening friends James McNair and Bob

This desertscape grows in a ten-inch unglazed pot saucer, one of the most readily accessible means of gardening in a bowl. Plant it as described on page 80. Photograph courtesy the Jackson & Perkins Co.

Springman. I call it the Tiffany Method, because Tiffany's is the store where they developed the technique. Here's the procedure:

Give the interior of the container a thick coating of petroleum jelly (Vaseline, for example), then place a large heavy-duty piece of polyethylene plastic (preferably clear and doubled if possible) inside. (The jelly will hold it in place.) Trim the plastic to fit the container, then proceed with planting. Stop the soil approximately one half to one inch from the top of the plastic. Mulch over the top with a ground cover plant or with florist sheet moss, small stones, bark chips or any other natural material that will not scratch the container where the plastic may not protect it.

Another possibility with a valuable bowl that you intend to use permanently as a planter is to have a jeweler bore drainage holes in the bottom. The drawback to this is that the bowl will then require a saucer to protect from moisture the surface on which it rests—and finding a saucer that will be aesthetically pleasing may be difficult. To me one of the chief advantages of waterproof bowl gardens is that they may be enjoyed anywhere indoors without much worry about moisture damage to the surface beneath.

Although I suggest sources for purchasing new containers, don't overlook the possibility of turning cracked or chipped glass, china or ceramic bowls into planters. Coating the interior with petroleum jelly and lining with plastic will prevent moisture seepage through any cracks, and the leaves of a plant may be placed to hide chips at the edge.

14   Geraniums in crystal cylinder

CONTAINER: Straight-sided glass fruit bowl, 6 inches deep by 12 inches in diameter. *Sources:* Department stores, usually with china and other glassware.

PLANTS: Common bedding geraniums.

SPECIAL PLANTING TECHNIQUE: Layer of gravel in bottom equal to approximately one third the height of the container, mixed with a handful of charcoal chips. Continue planting as if in ordinary clay flowerpot.

OWNER: James McNair.

ENVIRONMENT:

Light: As much direct sun as possible (half day minimum).

Temperature: Moderate in fall and winter (55–70° F.), average dwelling or office in spring and summer.

Humidity: Medium with fresh-air circulation.

Soil Mix: All-purpose (see Chapter One).

Soil Moisture: Evenly moist to slightly on the dry side.

Fertilizer: Make light applications of flowering house-plant fertilizer all year.

COMMENTS: Start with short young plants or rooted cuttings. Pinch out the growing tips as necessary to promote maximum branching and compact habit. Give plant a quarter turn in the same direction each time you water so that all parts receive an equal amount of sun.

Geraniums in crystal cylinder.

15   Miniature gloxinia in glass canister

CONTAINER: Food-storage canister with cover. *Source:* From Owens-Corning or similar manufacturer, usually with house-wares in department stores.

PLANT: *Sinningia pusilla* 'Snow White,' a miniature gloxinia. *Sources:* Plant shops or by mail from specialists (see Appendix).

SPECIAL PLANTING TECHNIQUE: Gloxinia grows in two-inch pot set in center of canister and surrounded by an inch-deep layer of sandstone pebbles. Green florist sheet moss hides the upper part of the pot.

OWNER: Author.

ENVIRONMENT:

Light: Bright, but little or no direct sun, or grow in a fluorescent-light garden.

Temperature: Moderate to warm, ideally a range of 65–75° F.

Humidity: High; seldom succeeds except in a closed terrarium.

Soil Mix: All-purpose (see Chapter One).

Soil Moisture: Evenly moist at all times.

Fertilizer: Make occasional, very light applications of flowering house-plant fertilizer all year.

COMMENTS: Use manicure scissors to trim off spent flowers and dead leaves.

Miniature gloxinia in glass canister.

16   Crystal bowl fern garden

CONTAINER: Crystal bowl 10 inches in diameter by 4 inches deep. *Sources:* Tiffany's provided the one shown; also with china and glassware in department stores.

PLANTS: Small maidenhair ferns (*Adiantum*), *Polystichum tsussimense* (a miniature fern) and trailing selaginella. *Sources:* Plant shops or by mail from specialists (see Appendix).

SPECIAL PLANTING TECHNIQUE: Place an inch-deep layer of pebbles in bottom, topped by a sprinkling of charcoal chips, then proceed with planting. Carpet bare ground with green woods moss.

OWNER: James McNair.

ENVIRONMENT:

Light: Bright, but little or no direct sun, or grow in a fluorescent-light garden.

Temperature: Moderate to warm, ideally a range of 60–75° F.

Humidity: Moderate to high; mist daily; protect from drafts of hot, dry air.

Soil Mix: All-purpose (see Chapter One).

Soil Moisture: Evenly moist at all times.

Fertilizer: Make occasional, very light applications of foliage-plant fertilizer all year.

COMMENTS: Use manicure scissors to remove any dead fronds. This bowl garden makes a wonderful dining-table centerpiece. For a touch of color, insert a florist water pick in the soil and place a small flower or two in it.

Crystal bowl fern garden.

17   Sweetmeat tree garden

CONTAINER: Crystal sweetmeat tree. *Source:* Tiffany's provided the one shown; also with china and glassware in department stores.

PLANTS: Selaginellas (shown); baby's-tears could be used to create a similar effect in a place where there was too much light and warmth and not enough humidity to suit the needs of the selaginella. *Sources:* Plant shops or from specialists (see Appendix).

SPECIAL PLANTING TECHNIQUE: Place a half-inch-deep layer of pebbles in bottom of each cup, topped by a sprinkling of charcoal chips, then proceed with planting. Carpet bare ground with green woods moss or tiny pebbles.

OWNER: James McNair.

ENVIRONMENT:

Light: Bright, but little or no direct sun.

Temperature: Moderate to high; mist daily; protect from drafts of hot, dry air.

Soil Mix: All-purpose (see Chapter One).

Soil Moisture: Evenly moist at all times.

Fertilizer: Make occasional, very light applications of foliage-plant fertilizer all year.

COMMENTS: A planted sweetmeat tree like this one can be put to countless decorative uses. If a bright window is not available, place the individual cups to grow in a fluorescent-light garden; remove and hang on the tree for special occasions. Some cups might contain miniature African violets, begonias or gloxinias, others could be filled with water and a few cut flowers.

Sweetmeat tree garden.

18   Stacked bowl garden

CONTAINERS: Stacked Japanese porcelain bowls. *Source:* Tiffany's provided the ones shown; also in specialty shops and department stores.

PLANT: Baby's-tears (*Soleirolia Soleirolii,* formerly known as *Helxine soleirolii*). *Sources:* Local shops or by mail from specialists (see Appendix).

SPECIAL PLANTING TECHNIQUE: Coat the interior with petroleum jelly, then line with heavy-duty polyethylene plastic. Add a half-inch layer of pebbles, topped by a sprinkling of charcoal chips, then proceed with planting. Carpet any bare soil at the surface with green woods moss, florist sheet moss or small stones.

OWNER: James McNair.

ENVIRONMENT:

Light: Bright, but little or no direct sun, or grow in a fluorescent-light garden.

Temperature: Moderate, ideally a range of 55–70° F.

Humidity: Moderate to high; mist daily; protect from drafts of hot, dry air.

Soil Mix: All-purpose (see Chapter One).

Soil Moisture: Evenly moist at all times.

Fertilizer: Make occasional, very light applications of foliage-plant fertilizer all year.

COMMENTS: Use scissors to keep wayward strands of growth trimmed neatly. A gardening friend of mine who lives in a high-rise apartment maintains several plantings of baby's-tears similar to this one which he "mows" regularly with scissors and refers to as his "lawns."

Stacked bowl garden.

19   Pothos in a bowl

CONTAINER: Glazed ceramic, oblong, about 10 by 6 by 5 inches deep. *Sources:* Department stores, usually with china and glass.

PLANT: Common pothos (*Epipremnum aureum,* formerly known as *Scindapsus aureus*). *Sources:* Wherever plants are sold locally or by mail (see Appendix).

SPECIAL PLANTING TECHNIQUE: Line bottom with an inch-deep layer of pebbles, topped by a sprinkling of charcoal chips, then proceed with planting. Carpet any bare soil at the surface with florist sheet moss.

OWNER: Author.

ENVIRONMENT:

Light: Bright, up to a half day of sun, or grow in a fluorescent-light garden.

Temperature: Average dwelling or office, ideally a range of 60–75° F.

Humidity: Moderate to high, but tolerates less; mist frequently to keep leaves rain-fresh.

Soil Mix: All-purpose (see Chapter One).

Soil Moisture: Evenly moist at all times.

Fertilizer: Make occasional, very light applications of foliage-plant fertilizer all year.

COMMENTS: Here is a perfect example of how the most ordinary of foliage plants can be turned into a beautiful garden simply by massing in a complementary container. Wayward new growth can be led back into the interior of the planting and held in place with a medium-size hairpin.

Pothos in a bowl.

20   Ming aralia in Chinese bowl

CONTAINER: Four-sided gray china bowl, 10 inches in diameter by 6 inches deep. *Source:* Tiffany's; less expensive bowls of similar shape are available in Japanese shops, Azuma in New York, for example; specialty stores in general, Crate and Barrel in Chicago, for example.

PLANTS: *Polyscias fruticosa* (ming aralia) with ground cover of *Sagina subulata* (pearlwort, sometimes called Irish or Scottish moss; it is in fact a relative of the dianthus or pink and not in any way related to true moss). *Sources:* Plant shops, nurseries or by mail (see Appendix).

SPECIAL PLANTING TECHNIQUE: Add an inch-deep layer of pebbles in the bottom, topped by a sprinkling of charcoal chips, then proceed with planting.

OWNER: James McNair.

ENVIRONMENT:

Light: Half day of direct sun.

Temperature: Average dwelling or office, ideally a range of 55–70° F. during the winter heating season.

Humidity: Medium with fresh-air circulation; mist frequently.

Soil Mix: All-purpose (see Chapter One).

Soil Moisture: Evenly moist to slightly on the dry side.

Fertilizer: Make occasional, light applications of foliage-plant fertilizer all year.

COMMENTS: Use scissors to keep the sagina ground cover low and tidy.

Ming aralia in Chinese bowl.

21   Silver bowl garden

CONTAINER: Sterling silver dolphin bowl. ˙ *Source:* Tiffany's provided the one shown; also in other jewelers, specialty shops, department stores.

PLANTS: Red-leaved *Iresine herbstii* surrounded by green and gold forms of baby's-tears (*Soleirolia Soleirolii*). *Sources:* Local shops or by mail from specialists (see Appendix).

SPECIAL PLANTING TECHNIQUE: Coat the interior with petroleum jelly, then line with heavy-duty polyethylene plastic. Add a half-inch layer of pebbles, topped by a sprinkling of charcoal chips, then proceed with planting, first positioning the iresine in the center, then surrounding it with baby's-tears.

CREATED BY: James McNair (who owns Catahoula Parish, the cat).

ENVIRONMENT:

Light: Half day of sun, or grow in a fluorescent-light garden.

Temperature: Average dwelling or office, ideally a range of 55–75° F.

Humidity: Moderate; mist frequently; needs fresh-air circulation, but protect from drafts of hot, dry air.

Soil Mix: All-purpose (see Chapter One).

Soil Moisture: Evenly moist at all times.

Fertilizer: Make occasional, very light applications of foliage-plant fertilizer all year.

COMMENTS: Prune back the iresine as necessary to keep it in scale with the rest of the planting. If cultivated in natural light, give the container a quarter turn in the same direction each time you water so that all parts will receive an equal amount of sun.

Silver bowl garden.

22   Coleus en casserole

CONTAINER: Copper casserole approximately 18 inches in diameter by 6 inches deep. *Source:* Department stores and gourmet cookware shops.

PLANTS: Common coleus. *Sources:* Wherever plants are sold, or by mail from specialists (see Appendix).

SPECIAL PLANTING TECHNIQUE: Coat the interior with petroleum jelly, then line with heavy-duty polyethylene plastic. Add an inch-deep layer of pebbles, topped by a sprinkling of charcoal chips, then proceed with planting.

OWNER: James McNair.

ENVIRONMENT:

Light: Half day or more of sun, or grow in a fluorescent-light garden.

Temperature: Average dwelling or office, ideally a range of 60–75° F.

Humidity: Low to high, but needs fresh-air circulation.

Soil Mix: All-purpose (see Chapter One).

Soil Moisture: Evenly moist to slightly on the dry side.

Fertilizer: Make occasional, very light applications of foliage-plant fertilizer all year.

COMMENTS: Pinch out the growing tips of all branches following every two or three inches of new growth. If cultivated in natural light, give the container a quarter turn counterclockwise each time you water so that all parts will receive an equal amount of sun.

Coleus en casserole.

23   Art deco vase gardens

CONTAINERS: Art deco vases. *Sources:* Antique shops, junk dealers, swap meets, tag sales.

PLANTS: Green-leaved *Crassula pseudolycopodioides* (left) grows in a green satin glass vase; almost-black-leaved *Aeonium arboreum atropurpureum* (right) grows in a black vase. *Sources:* Local shops, or by mail from specialists in cacti and other succulents (see Appendix).

SPECIAL PLANTING TECHNIQUE: Coat the interior with petroleum jelly, then line with heavy-duty polyethylene plastic. Add a two-inch layer of pebbles, topped by a sprinkling of charcoal chips, then proceed with planting. Carpet the surface with gravel or pebbles.

OWNER: James McNair.

ENVIRONMENT:

Light: Half day or more of sun, or grow four inches directly beneath the tubes in a fluorescent-light garden.

Temperature: Average dwelling or office.

Humidity: Low to medium with fresh-air circulation. Mist occasionally to keep plants dust-free.

Soil Mix: Cactus/succulent (see Chapter One).

Soil Moisture: Evenly moist to on the dry side.

Fertilizer: Make occasional, light applications of foliage-plant fertilizer in spring and summer only.

COMMENTS: If you have trouble deciding when to add water to deep, drainless containers like these, use the long probe of a soil moisture meter to determine moisture conditions down where the roots are.

Art deco vase gardens.

24   Shrimp plant creole

CONTAINER: Iron Dutch oven. *Sources:* Department stores and gourmet cookware shops.

PLANT: Shrimp plant (*Justicia Brandegeana,* formerly known as *Beloperone guttata*). *Sources:* Local shops or by mail from specialists (see Appendix).

SPECIAL PLANTING TECHNIQUE: To prevent rust, coat the interior with petroleum jelly, then line with heavy-duty polyethylene plastic. Add an inch-deep layer of pebbles, topped by a sprinkling of charcoal chips, then proceed with planting.

OWNER: James McNair (who also prepares a mean pot of shrimp creole).

ENVIRONMENT:

Light: Half day or more of direct sun, or grow in a fluorescent-light garden.

Temperature: Average dwelling or office, ideally a range of 60–75° F. in fall and winter.

Humidity: Medium with fresh-air circulation.

Soil Mix: All-purpose (see Chapter One).

Soil Moisture: Evenly moist to slightly on the dry side.

Fertilizer: Make occasional, light applications of flowering house-plant fertilizer all year.

COMMENTS: If you are growing shrimp plant in natural light, give the pot a quarter turn counterclockwise each time you water so that all parts will receive an equal amount of sun. Since shrimp plant blooms on new growth, prune back as necessary to maintain an attractive shape and size.

Shrimp plant creole.

25   Herb garden in wok

CONTAINER: Chinese iron wok. *Sources:* Department stores and gourmet cookware shops.

PLANTS: Basil, parsley, mint, dill, rosemary, marjoram, thyme, chives. *Sources:* Plant shops, nurseries, by mail from specialists (see Appendix).

SPECIAL PLANTING TECHNIQUE: To prevent rust, coat the interior with petroleum jelly, then line with heavy-duty polyethylene plastic. Add an inch-deep layer of pebbles in the bottom, topped by a sprinkling of charcoal chips, then proceed with planting.

OWNER: James McNair.

ENVIRONMENT:

Light: Half day or more of direct sun, or grow in a fluorescent-light garden.

Temperature: Average dwelling or office, ideally a range of 55–70° F. during the winter heating season.

Humidity: Medium with fresh-air circulation.

Soil Mix: All-purpose (see Chapter One).

Soil Moisture: Evenly moist to slightly on the dry side.

Fertilizer: Make occasional, light applications of foliage-plant fertilizer all year.

COMMENTS: If you grow this garden in natural light, give the wok a quarter turn counterclockwise each time you water so that all of the herbs will receive an equal amount of sun. If the leaves and stems you snip off for cooking aren't sufficient to maintain a tidy appearance, trim back periodically, simply to restore the order and beauty of the original planting.

Herb garden in wok.

CONTAINER: Octagonal-shaped silver bowl 15 inches in diameter by 4 inches deep. *Source:* Tiffany's provided the one shown; also in other jewelry stores, specialty shops, department stores.

PLANTS: Assorted young or small-growing ferns—maidenhair, Fluffy Ruffles and *Polystichum tsus-simense. Sources:* Local shops or by mail from specialists (see Appendix).

SPECIAL PLANTING TECHNIQUE: Coat the interior with petroleum jelly, then line with heavy-duty polyethylene plastic. Add a half-inch layer of pebbles, topped by a sprinkling of charcoal chips, then proceed with planting. Carpet any bare soil at the surface with green woods moss or florist sheet moss.

OWNER: James McNair.

ENVIRONMENT:

Light: Bright, but little or no direct sun, or grow in a fluorescent-light garden.

Temperature: Average dwelling or office, ideally a range of 55–75° F.

Humidity: Moderate to high; mist frequently; protect from drafts of hot, dry air.

Soil Mix: All-purpose (see Chapter One).

Soil Moisture: Evenly moist at all times.

Fertilizer: Make occasional, very light applications of foliage-plant fertilizer all year.

COMMENTS: An easily portable fernery like this one may be brought to the table and used as a centerpiece on almost countless occasions.

Silver bowl fernery.

27   Salad bowl garden

CONTAINER: Wood salad bowl. *Sources:* Department stores, gourmet cookware shops, your own kitchen.

PLANT: Caladium. *Sources:* Plant shops, nurseries, by mail (see Appendix).

SPECIAL PLANTING TECHNIQUE: Coat the interior with petroleum jelly, then line with heavy-duty polyethylene plastic to prevent moisture from harming wood. Add an inch-deep layer of pebbles in the bottom, topped by a sprinkling of charcoal chips, then proceed with planting.

OWNER: James McNair.

ENVIRONMENT:

Light: Half day of direct sun or grow in a fluorescent-light garden.

Temperature: Warm (65–80° F.) in spring and summer, during the active growing season; moderate (55–70° F.) in fall and winter while the tubers from which caladiums grow are in a state of dormancy.

Humidity: Medium to high with fresh-air circulation in spring and summer; of no consideration while dormant.

Soil Mix: All-purpose (see Chapter One).

Soil Moisture: Evenly moist in spring and summer, barely damp during dormancy in fall and winter.

Fertilizer: Make occasional, light applications of foliage-plant fertilizer in spring and summer only.

COMMENTS: Caladium leaves are poisonous, so don't let anyone get the bright idea of eating them just because they are growing in a salad bowl.

Salad bowl garden.

28   Green and white soufflé

CONTAINER: White soufflé dish, 10 inches in diameter by 5 inches deep. *Sources:* Department stores, gourmet cookware shops, your own kitchen.

PLANT: *Euonymus fortunei* 'Emerald Gaiety,' a small evergreen shrub of dense branching habit with a pronounced white margin on the dark green, rounded leaves. *Sources:* Local nurseries or by mail (see Appendix).

SPECIAL PLANTING TECHNIQUE: Add an inch-deep layer of pebbles in the bottom, topped by a sprinkling of charcoal chips, then proceed with planting. Carpet the soil surface with white gravel chips.

OWNER: James McNair.

ENVIRONMENT:

Light: Half day or more of direct sun, or grow in a fluorescent-light garden.

Temperature: Cool to moderate (40–70° F.) during the winter heating season; average dwelling or office in spring and summer.

Humidity: Medium with fresh-air circulation; mist frequently.

Soil Mix: All-purpose (see Chapter One).

Soil Moisture: Evenly moist at all times.

Fertilizer: Make occasional, light applications of foliage-plant fertilizer in spring and summer only.

COMMENTS: This bowl garden would make an excellent housewarming gift, since the recipient would have the option of enjoying it for a time as is, then planting the euonymus outdoors and reclaiming the soufflé dish for the kitchen.

Green and white soufflé.

29   Desertscape in clay-pot saucer

CONTAINER: Ordinary clay-pot saucer 9 inches in diameter. *Sources:* Plant shops, nurseries, garden centers.

PLANTS: (Left to right) elephant bush (portulacaria), *Euphorbia trigona,* a *Mammillaria* cactus and a young agave. *Sources:* Plant shops, nurseries or by mail (see Appendix).

SPECIAL PLANTING TECHNIQUE: None required. Simply remove plants from pots and crumble away most of the old soil, then position each in the saucer, spreading the roots over a layer of fresh soil and adding more on top so that they stand securely. Add finishing touches of builder's sand and pebble mulches, possibly with a "boulder" of Featherock, as shown.

OWNER: Bill Mulligan.

ENVIRONMENT:

Light: Half day or more of direct sun.

Temperature: Average dwelling or office.

Humidity: Low to medium with fresh-air circulation. Mist occasionally to keep plants dust-free.

Soil Mix: Cactus/succulent (see Chapter One).

Soil Moisture: Evenly moist to on the dry side.

Fertilizer: Make occasional, light applications of foliage-plant fertilizer in spring and summer only.

COMMENTS: This bowl garden can be enjoyed for several weeks at a time in relatively low light, but then it will go into decline unless returned to full sun.

Desertscape in clay-pot saucer.

30   Desertscape in pottery casserole

Except for the container (a pottery casserole 14 by 8 by 2 inches deep) and slight variation in the cacti and other succulents included, this bowl garden, from the collection of Bill Mulligan, is planted and maintained in exactly the same way as that shown in photograph on page 81.

Desertscape in pottery casserole.

Sometimes one plant, in this case a *Mammillaria* cactus in bloom, and the right container, here a shallow clay bowl, is all it takes to create a beautiful garden. For planting technique, see page 80.

31   Living succulents for hors d'oeuvre tray

CONTAINER: Plastic hors d'oeuvre tray with four half-circle compartments surrounding a square one. *Sources:* Department stores, gift shops, your own kitchen.

PLANTS: Assorted cacti and other succulents. *Sources:* Plant shops, nurseries or by mail (see Appendix).

SPECIAL PLANTING TECHNIQUE: Coat interior walls with petroleum jelly, then line with heavy-duty polyethylene plastic (this is to prevent scratches in the container). Add an inch-deep layer of pebbles in the bottom, topped by a sprinkling of charcoal chips, then proceed with planting. Carpet any bare soil

Living succulents for hors d'oeuvre tray.

with sand, pebbles or broken clay-pot shards hammered into small chips.

OWNER: James McNair.

ENVIRONMENT:

Light: Half day or more of direct sun, or grow four inches directly beneath the tubes in a fluorescent-light garden.

Temperature: Average dwelling or office.

Humidity: Low to medium with fresh-air circulation. Mist occasionally to keep plants dust-free.

Soil Mix: Cactus/succulent (see Chapter One).

Soil Moisture: Evenly moist to on the dry side.

Fertilizer: Make occasional, light applications of foliage-plant fertilizer in spring and summer only.

COMMENTS: This low-profile bowl garden is ideal as a table centerpiece, but don't leave it in low light for more than a few days at a time.

32   Tray chic desertscape

CONTAINER: Plastic silverware drawer organizer. *Sources:* Dime, department, hardware and discount stores, your own kitchen.

PLANTS: Assorted small cacti and other succulents. *Sources:* Plant shops, nurseries, by mail (see Appendix).

SPECIAL PLANTING TECHNIQUE: Add single layer of pebbles in bottom and sprinkle with charcoal chips, then proceed with planting. Add an interesting rock or two, but leave some open spaces. Carpet the surface with sand and pebbles, alternating from one compartment to another.

OWNER: Bill Mulligan.

ENVIRONMENT:

Light: Half day or more of direct sun, or grow four inches directly beneath the tubes in a fluorescent-light garden.

Temperature: Average dwelling or office.

Humidity: Low to medium with fresh-air circulation. Mist occasionally to keep plants dust-free.

Soil Mix: Cactus/succulent (see Chapter One).

Soil Moisture: Evenly moist to on the dry side.

Fertilizer: Make occasional, light applications of foliage-plant fertilizer in spring and summer only.

COMMENTS: Even if you have to buy the plants, this bowl garden makes an inexpensive gift that may be of untold value to the person who receives it, especially if he or she is housebound, owing to advanced age or illness.

Tray chic desertscape.

33   Washtub garden

CONTAINER: Miniature galvanized metal washtub. *Sources:* Dime, department or hardware stores.

PLANTS: Assorted small cacti or other succulents. *Sources:* Plant shops, nurseries, by mail (see Appendix).

SPECIAL PLANTING TECHNIQUE: Add half-inch layer of pebbles in bottom and sprinkle with charcoal chips, then proceed with planting. If you like, punch a few drainage holes in the bottom, using a hammer and nail; however, it will then require some kind of saucer to catch excess moisture.

OWNER: James McNair.

ENVIRONMENT:

Light: Half day or more of direct sun, or grow four inches directly beneath the tubes in a fluorescent-light garden.

Temperature: Average dwelling or office.

Humidity: Low to medium with fresh-air circulation. Mist occasionally to keep plants dust-free.

Soil Mix: Cactus/succulent (see Chapter One).

Soil Moisture: Evenly moist to on the dry side.

Fertilizer: Make occasional, light applications of foliage-plant fertilizer in spring and summer only.

COMMENTS: If you have trouble handling thorny cacti at transplanting time, try this: Fold a sheet of newspaper into a long strip about an inch wide; wrap this around the cactus and grip the ends together. Or, if the cactus is small enough, hold it with scissors-type kitchen tongs.

Washtub garden.

34   Gelatin mold desert garden

CONTAINER: Tin gelatin mold. *Sources:* Department stores and gourmet cookware shops, maybe your own kitchen if you've given up preparing aspic.

PLANTS: Young specimens of *Crassula falcata. Sources:* Plant shops, nurseries or by mail from specialists in cacti and other succulents (see Appendix).

SPECIAL PLANTING TECHNIQUE: Coat the interior with petroleum jelly, then line with heavy-duty polyethylene plastic to guard against rust. Add a half-inch layer of pebbles, topped by a sprinkling of charcoal chips, then proceed with planting. Carpet the surface with gravel.

OWNER: James McNair.

ENVIRONMENT:

Light: Half day or more of sun, or grow four inches directly beneath the tubes in a fluorescent-light garden.

Temperature: Average dwelling or office.

Humidity: Low to medium with fresh-air circulation. Mist occasionally to keep plants dust-free.

Soil Mix: Cactus/succulent (see Chapter One).

Soil Moisture: Evenly moist to on the dry side.

Fertilizer: Make occasional, light applications of foliage-plant fertilizer in spring and summer only.

COMMENTS: Here is another bowl garden that makes an almost fail-safe apartment or housewarming gift. If the recipient proves to be the kiss of death to flora, maybe he or she will clean up the mold and make delicious aspic.

Gelatin mold desert garden.

35   Tin pâté mold

CONTAINER: Tin pâté mold. *Sources:* Department stores and gourmet cookware shops.

PLANTS: Strawberry-begonia (*Saxifraga stolonifera*) surrounded by baby's-tears (*Soleirolia Soleirolii*). *Sources:* Local shops or by mail from specialists (see Appendix).

SPECIAL PLANTING TECHNIQUE: Coat the interior with petroleum jelly, then line with heavy-duty polyethylene plastic. Add a half-inch-deep layer of pebbles, topped by a sprinkling of charcoal chips, then proceed with planting.

OWNER: James McNair.

ENVIRONMENT:

Light: Bright or a few hours of sun, or grow in a fluorescent-light garden.

Temperature: Average dwelling or office, ideally a range of 60–75° F.

Humidity: Medium, with fresh-air circulation; mist frequently; protect from drafts of hot, dry air.

Soil Mix: All-purpose (see Chapter One).

Soil Moisture: Evenly moist at all times.

Fertilizer: Make occasional, very light applications of foliage-plant fertilizer all year.

COMMENTS: A bowl garden like this one can be kept in fine form for as many as two years. It would also make an unusual gift for anyone who likes plants or who is seriously into cooking.

Tin pâté mold.

36   The layered look

CONTAINERS: Square glass battery jars. *Sources:* Laboratory supply houses or with china and glassware in department stores.

PLANTS: Only the ponytail (*Beaucarnea recurvata*) in the center container is growing in soil; the sweet potato vine (left) and coleus (right) are growing in water. *Sources:* Plant shops, nurseries or by mail from specialists (see Appendix).

SPECIAL PLANTING TECHNIQUE: The idea here is to take advantage of the visibility glass affords to show off the roots of the plant as well as layers of different natural planting mediums, placed so as to represent a geological cross section of the earth's surface.

OWNER: James McNair.

First assemble the ingredients: gravel, charcoal chips, coarse sand, peat moss, fine sand and potting soil.

Add one layer at a time, keeping lines uneven and flowing; contrast colors and textures from layer to layer.

Allow space at the top for roots and soil; firm in place.

ENVIRONMENT:

Light: Half day or more of sun.

Temperature: Average dwelling or office.

Humidity: Low to medium with fresh-air circulation. Mist occasionally to keep plants dust-free.

Soil Mix: All-purpose (see Chapter One).

Soil Moisture: Evenly moist to on the dry side.

Fertilizer: Make occasional, light applications of foliage-plant fertilizer in spring and summer only.

COMMENTS: To grow plants in water, like the sweet potato and coleus illustrated here, simply add fresh as necessary to keep all roots submerged. Once a month pour out the old water and refill with fresh, first adding a quarter teaspoon of foliage-plant fertilizer to each quart.

The layered look.

37   **Crystal Palace bowl garden**

CONTAINER: Cut crystal in rectangular brick pattern. *Sources:* Tiffany's provided the one shown; also from other jewelry stores, specialty shops, with china and glassware in department stores.

PLANT: Pilea species. *Sources:* Plant shops, nurseries or by mail from specialists (see Appendix). Any of the dwarf vines and trailers listed in the Appendix might be used instead.

SPECIAL PLANTING TECHNIQUE: Same as for the layered look, page 94.

OWNER: James McNair.

ENVIRONMENT:

Light: Up to a half day of sun, or grow in a fluorescent-light garden.

Temperature: Average dwelling or office.

Humidity: Medium, with fresh-air circulation; mist frequently.

Soil Mix: All-purpose (see Chapter One).

Soil Moisture: Evenly moist at all times.

Fertilizer: Make occasional, light applications of foliage-plant fertilizer all year.

COMMENTS: This is an excellent way to grow and display a small trailing plant without having to hang it.

Crystal Palace bowl garden.

38   Living bouquet garden

CONTAINER: Laboratory desiccator jar, approximately ten inches in diameter and as tall. *Sources:* Laboratory supply houses.

PLANT: Mid-century hybrid lily. *Sources:* Plant shops, nurseries, garden centers or purchase the bulbs by mail (see Appendix).

SPECIAL PLANTING TECHNIQUE: Same as for the layered look (see page 94). Plant dormant bulbs three inches deep in late fall or early winter. Place to root in a dark, cool place (35–45° F.) for eight to twelve weeks, then bring to light and warmth for growing on.

OWNER: James McNair.

ENVIRONMENT:

Light: Half day or more of sun.

Temperature: Cool until roots form (see above); moderate thereafter (55–70° F.).

Humidity: Medium to high, with fresh-air circulation.

Soil Mix: All-purpose (see Chapter One).

Soil Moisture: Evenly moist at all times.

Fertilizer: Make occasional, light applications of flowering-plant fertilizer in late winter and spring after growth becomes active.

COMMENTS: If you don't want to go to the trouble of growing your own lilies from the dormant bulbs, purchase a pot or two already in bud and transplant to a decorative container with as little disturbance to the roots as possible. When flowers fade, transplant bulbs to a permanent place in the garden.

Living bouquet garden.

39   Miniature "rooftop" gardens

CONTAINERS: Square battery jars. *Sources:* Laboratory supply houses or with china and glassware in department stores.

PLANTS: Green and gold forms of baby's-tears (*Soleirolia Soleirolii*). *Sources:* Plant shops, nurseries or by mail (see Appendix).

SPECIAL PLANTING TECHNIQUE: Same as for the layered look (see page 94).

OWNERS: James McNair (and Catahoula Parish, shown inspecting the gardens).

ENVIRONMENT:

Light: Up to a half day of sun, or grow in a fluorescent-light garden.

Temperature: Average dwelling or office.

Humidity: Medium to high, with fresh-air circulation.

Soil Mix: All-purpose (see Chapter One).

Soil Moisture: Evenly moist at all times.

Fertilizer: Make occasional, light applications of foliage-plant fertilizer all year.

COMMENTS: Use scissors to trim back any unruly growth.

Miniature "rooftop" gardens.

40   Bromeliads on the half shell

CONTAINER: Seashell with encrustations; any seashell large enough to plant in. *Sources:* Along any shore, ideally at low tide.

PLANTS: Miniature tillandsias, which are bromeliads closely related to Spanish moss as well as the pineapple we eat. *Sources:* Plant shops or by mail from specialists (see Appendix).

SPECIAL PLANTING TECHNIQUE: Place shell in pan and cover with cold water; bring to boil and simmer for fifteen minutes. Pour off water and allow to cool. Immediately clean out the remains of any creature that may recently have lived in the shell, then proceed with planting. Wrap the roots of each bromeliad in enough unmilled sphagnum moss so that it will fit snugly in the shell opening.

OWNER: Nadine Zimet.

ENVIRONMENT:

Light: Up to a half day of sun, or grow in a fluorescent-light garden.

Temperature: Average dwelling or office.

Humidity: Medium to high, with fresh-air circulation; mist twice daily.

Soil Mix: Unmilled sphagnum moss (see above).

Soil Moisture: Evenly moist to on the dry side. To moisten, immerse entire planting in tepid water for two or three minutes, then remove and allow to drain before returning to the growing area.

Fertilizer: Mist leaves with foliar fertilizer, diluted in water according to directions on the label, once a month.

COMMENTS: Any of the cryptanthus or earth-star bromeliads also make excellent choices for shell planters.

Bromeliads on the half shell.

41   Narcissus bowl garden

CONTAINER: Chinese porcelain bowl about 8 inches in diameter by 2 inches deep. *Sources:* Antique dealers, with china and glassware in department stores, swap meets, tag sales.

PLANTS: Paperwhite narcissus (shown) or the golden Soleil d'Or form. *Sources:* Local garden centers and nurseries in autumn, or by mail from bulb specialists (see Appendix).

SPECIAL PLANTING TECHNIQUE: Fill bowl to within a half inch of the rim with pebbles or gravel. Snuggle the base of each bulb into the surface up to an inch deep. Fill bowl with water. Place to root in a dark, cool (50–60° F.) place for three or four weeks; check from time to time and add water as necessary. When well-rooted, bring to light and more warmth.

OWNER: Jacqueline Heriteau.

ENVIRONMENT:

Light: Up to a half day of sun.

Temperature: Cool until rooted (see above), then moderate (50–70° F.).

Humidity: Medium to high, with fresh-air circulation.

Soil Mix: Pebbles or gravel.

Soil Moisture: See above.

Fertilizer: None required.

COMMENTS: After the flowers fade, cut off the stems. Continue adding water to the pebbles until the leaves begin to turn yellow, then discard. (If you live in the Deep South, narcissus bulbs of this type may be planted in the garden, but do not try to force the same ones again indoors.)

Narcissus bowl garden.

42   Edible bowl gardens

CONTAINERS: Shallow glass ashtrays, coasters or laboratory ware. *Sources:* Laboratory supply houses, with china and glassware in department stores, swap meets, tag and garage sales.

PLANTS: Seeds for sprouting—mung bean, alfalfa, wheat. *Sources:* Health food stores.

SPECIAL PLANTING TECHNIQUE: Scatter seeds thickly on the bottom of each container; add about a quarter inch of water; place to sprout in a dark, warm place, a kitchen cabinet for example. As soon as sprouting is evident, take to the light.

OWNER: James McNair.

ENVIRONMENT:

Light: Darkness at first (see above), then take to bright light but little or no direct sun.

Temperature: Average dwelling or office.

Humidity: Medium, with fresh-air circulation after sprouting.

Soil Mix: Use water only (see above).

Soil Moisture: After sprouting, add fresh water daily, first pouring off most of the old.

Fertilizer: None required.

COMMENTS: These little sprout gardens will last only a few days even if you don't eat them in salads and sandwiches. However, they are fun to watch and their fresh green is an encouraging sight, especially in the dead of winter.

Edible bowl gardens.

43   Redwood burl garden

CONTAINER: Chinese bowl about 8 inches in diameter by 3 inches deep. *Sources:* Antique dealers or with china and glassware in department stores.

PLANT: Redwood burl. *Sources:* By mail from specialists (see Appendix).

SPECIAL PLANTING TECHNIQUE: Place burl, flat side down, in bowl and add about a half inch of water.

OWNER: Francesca Morris.

ENVIRONMENT:

Light: Up to a half day of sun, or grow in a fluorescent-light garden.

Temperature: Average dwelling or office, ideally not above 70° F. in winter.

Humidity: Medium to high with fresh-air circulation. After the burl sprouts, mist daily.

Soil Mix: Use water only (see above).

Soil Moisture: Drain off old water, clean bowl and rinse burl, then replace with fresh water once a week.

Fertilizer: None required.

COMMENTS: With faithful care as described above, a redwood burl may remain healthy and green for a year or more.

Redwood burl garden.

44   Ming jar water garden

CONTAINER: Crystal ming jar. *Sources:* Tiffany's provided the one shown; less expensive copies may be found with china and glassware in department stores and in specialty shops.

PLANTS: Various aquatics sold for aquariums. *Sources:* Pet shops or by mail from water-lily specialists (see Appendix).

SPECIAL PLANTING TECHNIQUE: Anchor roots in an inch or two of pebbles that have been thoroughly washed in fresh water beforehand. Add a shell or two if you like.

OWNER: James McNair.

ENVIRONMENT:

Light: Bright, but little or no direct sun; may also be grown in a fluorescent-light garden.

Temperature: Average dwelling or office.

COMMENTS: Aerate daily by removing lid for several hours. Change water about once a month; trim back growth as necessary to maintain tidy appearance.

Ming jar water garden.

45   Half-barrel water garden

CONTAINER: Half barrel (wood construction). *Sources:* Distilleries or water-lily specialists (see Appendix).

PLANTS: Small-growing water lilies, other aquatics and bog plants each in their own pots. *Sources:* Water-lily specialists (see Appendix).

SPECIAL PLANTING TECHNIQUE: If the wood barrel has been used for wine, whiskey or olives, paint the inside with black plastic cement and cure thoroughly before using. Otherwise, fill the barrel with water and stir in a cup of lime (to neutralize the wood); let stand for five days, empty and refill with fresh water. Proceed with planting. Position aquatics six to twelve inches deep, bog types only one inch deep in the water. Add a pair of goldfish; they're fun to watch and good protection against mosquitoes taking up residence in your lily pond.

OWNER: Longwood Gardens, Kennett Square, Pennsylvania.

ENVIRONMENT:

Light: Half day or more of sun.

Temperature: Warm (65–80° F.) in spring and summer, cool (40–55° F.) in fall and winter.

Humidity: Medium to high with fresh-air circulation.

Soil Mix: Follow recommendations of the grower from whom you buy the plants.

Soil Moisture: Add fresh water to the barrel as necessary to replace that which evaporates.

Fertilizer: None required, unless specified by the grower from whom you purchase the plants.

COMMENTS: A typical half barrel holds twenty-five gallons of water and is therefore quite heavy. I suggest this bowl garden only for a terrace, patio or other place outdoors, or for a home greenhouse. In climates where winter temperatures drop below 40° F., a water garden like this one might be carried over in a frost-free garage, basement or other protected place.

Half-barrel water garden.

FOUR

Hiding pots with decorative containers that may not be waterproof

The bowl gardens in this chapter consist of one or more potted plants placed inside a container that is not waterproof, or might be damaged by prolonged exposure to moisture. While any one of these might be used outdoors for a special occasion, or for a brief period during dry weather, I do not recommend any of these containers for long-time exposure to the elements.

1. Line the inside with a sheet of heavy-duty polyethylene plastic; place a fairly deep waterproof saucer in the bottom.

2. Trim off the plastic even with the rim of the container.

3. Slip potted plant inside and carpet the surface with florist sheet moss.

46   Juniper in basket

CONTAINER: Inexpensive woven basket. *Sources:* Department stores, basket and plant shops.

PLANT: Dwarf juniper. *Sources:* Local nurseries or by mail from specialists (see Appendix).

SPECIAL PLANTING TECHNIQUE: Line basket with heavy-duty polyethylene plastic, add deep waterproof saucer, set potted plant inside and carpet surface with moss.

OWNER: James McNair.

ENVIRONMENT:

Light: Half day or more of sun.

Temperature: Cold to cool in fall and winter (28–50° F.), average dwelling, office or garden in other seasons.

Humidity: Medium to high, but always needs fresh air. Mist frequently while indoors.

Soil Mix: All-purpose (see Chapter One).

Soil Moisture: Evenly moist at all times.

Fertilizer: Make light applications in spring and summer only.

COMMENTS: Hardy evergreens like this one cannot long survive dry heat indoors in the winter. As container plants they are best wintered over outdoors in a coldframe, pit greenhouse or other protected place.

Juniper in basket.

47   **Pompon juniper in basket**

CONTAINER: Woven basket. *Sources:* Department stores, basket and plant shops.

PLANT: Dwarf juniper with so-called poodle cut. *Sources:* Local nurseries or by mail from specialists (see Appendix).

SPECIAL PLANTING TECHNIQUE: First line basket with florist sheet moss, right side facing out, then add plastic liner and place deep waterproof saucer inside, followed by the potted plant. Carpet the surface with more moss.

OWNER: James McNair.

ENVIRONMENT:

Light: Half day or more of sun.

Temperature: Cold to cool in fall and winter (28–50° F.), average dwelling, office or garden in other seasons.

Humidity: Medium to high, but always needs fresh air. Mist frequently while indoors.

Soil Mix: All-purpose (see Chapter One).

Soil Moisture: Evenly moist at all times.

Fertilizer: Make light applications in spring and summer only.

COMMENTS: Shear new growth as necessary to maintain the pompon cut. If you can't find a juniper already trained this way, purchase a bushy one and do the cutting yourself.

Pompon juniper in basket.

48   Baby's-tears, stage center

CONTAINER: Inexpensive woven basket. *Sources:* Department stores, basket and plant shops.

PLANT: Baby's-tears (*Soleirolia Soleirolii*). *Sources:* Plant shops, nurseries or by mail (see Appendix).

SPECIAL PLANTING TECHNIQUE: Line basket with heavy-duty polyethylene plastic, add deep waterproof saucer and set potted plant inside.

OWNER: Lawrence Wood.

ENVIRONMENT:

Light: Up to a half day of sun, a fluorescent-light garden, or grow under a seventy-five-watt incandescent grow light burned six to twelve hours daily, as shown.

Temperature: Average dwelling or office.

Humidity: Medium to high, with fresh air. Mist frequently.

Soil Mix: All-purpose (see Chapter One).

Soil Moisture: Evenly moist at all times.

Fertilizer: Make light applications of foliage-plant fertilizer all year.

COMMENTS: Baby's-tears may be treated as a miniature lawn; keep it tidy by "mowing" occasionally with scissors.

Baby's-tears, stage center.

49   Mushroom basket gardens

CONTAINERS: Mushroom baskets. *Sources:* Greengrocers, restaurants or among refuse placed at the curb for pickup in front of such establishments.

PLANTS: Polyanthus primroses and English daisies (*Bellis*). *Sources:* Local nurseries, garden centers and plant shops in winter or early spring.

SPECIAL PLANTING TECHNIQUE: Line basket with heavy-duty polyethylene plastic, add layer of pebbles or gravel for drainage, then proceed with planting. Remove daisies and primroses from the pots or flats in which you have purchased them and plant directly in the baskets. Carpet the surface with florist sheet moss.

OWNER: Author; shown in table setting at Royal Copenhagen's retail store in New York.

ENVIRONMENT:

Light: Up to a half day of sun or maintain in a fluorescent-light garden while not being used decoratively.

Temperature: Cool to moderate for growing (40–70° F.). Warmer temperatures will wither the flowers rapidly.

Humidity: Medium to high, with fresh air. Mist frequently.

Soil Mix: All-purpose (see Chapter One).

Soil Moisture: Evenly moist at all times.

Fertilizer: None required while in basket planting.

COMMENTS: When the last flowers fade, transplant to shaded, moist place outdoors in the garden.

Mushroom basket gardens.

50   Cycad in Ethiopian basket

CONTAINER: Red and black basket from Ethiopia. *Sources:* Department stores, basket and plant shops.

PLANT: *Cycas revoluta,* a cycad. *Sources:* Plant shops or by mail from specialists (see Appendix).

SPECIAL PLANTING TECHNIQUE: Line basket with heavy-duty polyethylene plastic, add deep waterproof saucer and set potted cycad inside. Carpet the surface with black polished stones.

OWNER: James McNair.

ENVIRONMENT:

Light: Half day of sun.

Temperature: Moderate (55–70° F.) in fall and winter, average dwelling or office in other seasons.

Humidity: Medium to high, with fresh-air circulation. Mist frequently.

Soil Mix: All-purpose (see Chapter One).

Soil Moisture: Evenly moist in spring and summer, evenly moist to slightly on the dry side in fall and winter.

Fertilizer: Make light applications of foliage-plant fertilizer in spring and summer only.

COMMENTS: Cycas is one of the oldest plants in cultivation; it dates from the time of the dinosaurs.

Cycad in Ethiopian basket.

51   Succulent in Mexican basket

CONTAINER: Woven straw basket from Mexico. *Sources:* Department stores, basket and plant shops.

PLANT: Hybrid echeveria. *Sources:* Plant shops or by mail from specialists in cacti and other succulents (see Appendix).

SPECIAL PLANTING TECHNIQUE: Line basket with heavy-duty polyethylene plastic, add deep waterproof saucer and set potted echeveria inside.

OWNER: James McNair.

ENVIRONMENT:

Light: Half day or more of sun or grow in a fluorescent-light garden about four inches directly beneath the tubes.

Temperature: Average dwelling or office.

Humidity: Low to medium, with fresh-air circulation.

Soil Mix: All-purpose or Cactus/succulent (see Chapter One).

Soil Moisture: Evenly moist to on the dry side.

Fertilizer: Make light applications of foliage-plant fertilizer in spring and summer only.

COMMENTS: An echeveria like this may be used decoratively in areas of relatively low light for a few days at a time, but then it should be moved back to a brighter spot.

Succulent in Mexican basket.

52   Jungle in basket

CONTAINER: Inexpensive woven basket, rectangular in shape, with a handle (obscured by the foliage). *Sources:* Department stores, basket and plant shops.

PLANTS: Coleus, a justicia with yellow bracts and white flowers, chlorophytum (spider plant), maranta (prayer plant), dieffenbachia (dumb cane) and aglaonema (Chinese evergreen).

SPECIAL PLANTING TECHNIQUE: Line basket with heavy-duty polyethylene plastic; add layer of pebbles or gravel in bottom for drainage. Remove plants from individual pots and replant in the basket, adding fresh soil as necessary to fill.

OWNER: Longwood Gardens, Kennett Square, Pennsylvania.

ENVIRONMENT:

Light: Half day or more of sun.

Temperature: Average dwelling or office.

Humidity: Medium to high, with fresh-air circulation. Mist frequently.

Soil Mix: All-purpose (see Chapter One).

Soil Moisture: Evenly moist at all times.

Fertilizer: Fertilize lightly all year.

COMMENTS: Success with a mixed planting like this one depends on combining plants whose cultural needs are compatible and regular grooming to keep dead leaves and flowers removed. Prune back as necessary to maintain a tidy appearance.

Jungle in basket.

53   Hollow-log planter

CONTAINER: A piece of log, partly decayed and hollowed out to form a planter. *Sources:* On the ground in a wooded area or along a stream.

PLANTS: Cattleya orchid and miniature fern (*Polystichum tsussimense*). *Sources:* Plant shops or by mail (see Appendix).

SPECIAL PLANTING TECHNIQUE: Line interior with heavy-duty polyethylene plastic. Place orchid pot inside and set small pot in which the fern grows on surface of orchid-growing medium.

OWNER: Longwood Gardens, Kennett Square, Pennsylvania.

ENVIRONMENT (for display only):

Light: Bright, little or no direct sun.

Temperature: Moderate (55–70° F.).

Humidity: Medium to high with fresh-air circulation. Mist frequently.

Soil Mix: Osmunda fiber for orchid; All-purpose for fern.

Soil Moisture: Evenly moist at all times while in display.

Fertilizer: None required while in this display.

COMMENTS: Orchids in general are not suited to cultivation in any kind of drainless container. However, I found this planting so attractive, I thought it an idea worth including. A similar container could serve as the permanent home for ferns, marantas, calatheas and countless other tropical foliage and flowering plants.

Hollow-log planter.

54   Purple passion in wire basket

CONTAINER: Wire basket. *Sources:* Department stores or shops that sell gourmet cookware, baskets or plants.

PLANT: *Gynura aurantiaca* (purple passion). *Sources:* Plant shops or by mail (see Appendix).

SPECIAL PLANTING TECHNIQUE: Line basket with florist sheet moss, right side facing out, then add plastic liner and place deep waterproof saucer inside, followed by the potted plant. Carpet the surface with more moss.

OWNER: James McNair.

ENVIRONMENT:

Light: Half day or more of sun, or grow in a fluorescent-light garden.

Temperature: Average dwelling or office.

Humidity: Medium with fresh-air circulation.

Soil Mix: All-purpose (see Chapter One).

Soil Moisture: Evenly moist to slightly on the dry side.

Fertilizer: Make light applications all year.

COMMENTS: Pinch back frequently to encourage compact growth, otherwise purple passion rapidly takes on an unkempt appearance.

Purple passion in wire basket.

55   Antique pot for cactus

CONTAINER: One-of-a-kind footed pre-Columbian pot. *Source:* Stendahl Galleries, Los Angeles.

PLANT: Globe-form cactus. *Sources:* Plant shops or by mail from cactus/succulent specialists (see Appendix).

SPECIAL PLANTING TECHNIQUE: Place waterproof saucer in bottom, then slip potted cactus inside.

OWNER: James McNair.

ENVIRONMENT:

Light: Half day or more of sun.

Temperature: Average dwelling or office.

Humidity: Low with fresh-air circulation.

Soil Mix: Cactus/succulent (Chapter One).

Soil Moisture: Evenly moist to slightly on the dry side in spring and summer; on the dry side in fall and winter.

Fertilizer: Make light applications in spring and summer only.

COMMENTS: This container would probably not be harmed by planting directly in it; however, the cactus itself is likely to grow better in a standard clay pot.

Antique pot for cactus.

56   Berry basket gardens

CONTAINERS: Sterling silver and wood berry baskets. *Sources:* Silver from Tiffany's, other jewelry stores, or with silver in department stores; wood from greengrocer.

PLANTS: Variegated strawberry-begonia in silver, plain in wood. *Sources:* Plant shops, nurseries or by mail (see Appendix). The Latin name for this plant is *Saxifraga stolonifera;* it is also called strawberry-geranium, but is in no way related to the fruit we eat, to begonias or to geraniums.

SPECIAL PLANTING TECHNIQUE: Fill corners with florist sheet moss, right side facing out, add heavy-duty polyethylene plastic liner and place layer of drainage pebbles in bottom, then proceed with planting. Carpet the surface with more moss.

OWNER: James McNair.

ENVIRONMENT:

Light: Up to a half day of sun, or grow in a fluorescent-light garden.

Temperature: Moderate in fall and winter (55–70° F.), average dwelling or office in other seasons.

Humidity: Medium to high with fresh-air circulation. Mist frequently.

Soil Mix: All-purpose (see Chapter One).

Soil Moisture: Evenly moist at all times.

Fertilizer: Make light applications all year.

COMMENTS: Bowl gardens like these make wonderful table centerpieces, perhaps with real strawberries added for decorative effect (and for your guests to eat if they like).

Berry basket gardens.

57   Basket for kangaroo vine

CONTAINER: Choctaw Indian basket. *Sources:* Department stores, basket or plant shops.

PLANT: *Cissus antarctica* (kangaroo vine). *Sources:* Plant shops or by mail (see Appendix).

SPECIAL PLANTING TECHNIQUE: Line basket with heavy-duty polyethylene plastic, add deep waterproof saucer, set potted plant inside and carpet surface with moss.

OWNER: James McNair.

ENVIRONMENT:

Light: Bright or up to a half day of sun.

Temperature: Average dwelling or office.

Humidity: Medium with fresh-air circulation. Mist frequently to keep leaves shiny clean.

Soil Mix: All-purpose (see Chapter One).

Soil Moisture: Evenly moist to slightly on the dry side.

Fertilizer: Make light applications all year.

COMMENTS: Here is an excellent example of an ordinary plant turned into a specimen of extraordinary beauty simply by mating it with a choice, complementary container.

Basket for kangaroo vine.

58   **Fernery in basket**

CONTAINERS: Woven baskets with matching lids, used here as decorative accessories. *Sources:* Department stores, basket and plant shops.

PLANTS: Assorted young or small-growing ferns and selaginellas. *Sources:* Plant shops or by mail from specialists (see Appendix).

SPECIAL PLANTING TECHNIQUE: Line baskets with heavy-duty polyethylene plastic, add a layer of pebbles for drainage, then proceed to plant directly in them. Carpet the surface with moss.

OWNER: Author.

ENVIRONMENT:

Light: Bright with brief periods of sun, or grow in a fluorescent-light garden.

Temperature: Moderate (55–70° F.) in fall and winter, average dwelling or office in other seasons.

Humidity: Medium to high. Mist frequently to keep the leaves rain-fresh.

Soil Mix: All-purpose (see Chapter One).

Soil Moisture: Evenly moist at all times.

Fertilizer: Make light applications all year.

COMMENTS: Small ferns and selaginellas in individual pots are hard to manage in most dwellings and offices because they dry out too quickly. When grouped in a basket as these are it is much easier to maintain properly moist soil.

Fernery in basket.

CONTAINER: Bark planter. *Sources:* Basket and plant shops, or fashion your own by hollowing out one end of a length of tree trunk.

PLANT: Asparagus-fern. *Sources:* Wherever plants are sold.

SPECIAL PLANTING TECHNIQUE: Line planter with heavy-duty polyethylene plastic, place deep waterproof saucer in bottom and slip potted asparagus-fern inside. Carpet the surface with florist sheet moss.

OWNER: James McNair.

ENVIRONMENT:

Light: Half day or more of sun.

Temperature: Average dwelling or office, but protect from drafts of hot, dry air in winter.

Humidity: Medium to high with fresh-air circulation. Mist frequently.

Soil Mix: All-purpose (see Chapter One).

Soil Moisture: Evenly moist at all times.

Fertilizer: Make light applications all year.

COMMENT: A tall planter like this is an excellent way to grow and display asparagus-fern without having to hang it from a wall bracket or ceiling hook.

Asparagus-fern in bark planter.

60   Growing arrangement in gardener's workbasket

CONTAINER: A Dicker Trug gardener's workbasket is shown. *Source:* Walter Nicke (see Appendix); any basket of similar depth might be used instead.

PLANTS: (Left to right) calathea, Easter cactus in bloom, cut daffodils, red-flowered calceolaria (pocketbook plant), blue-flowered streptocarpus and silver-leaved rex begonias. *Sources:* Plant shops or by mail (see Appendix).

SPECIAL PLANTING TECHNIQUE: Line basket with heavy-duty polyethylene plastic, then proceed to position plants inside, leaving them in their own pots. Use wads of unmilled sphagnum moss and chunks of osmunda fiber to prop and hold everything in place. Place daffodils or other cut flowers in bottles of water which can be hidden by foliage or pieces of moss.

OWNER: Author.

ENVIRONMENT (for display only):

Light: Bright, but little or no direct sun.

Temperature: Moderate (55–70° F.) to prolong the life of the flowers.

Humidity: Medium to high with fresh-air circulation. Mist frequently.

Soil Mix: All-purpose (see Chapter One).

Soil Moisture: Evenly moist at all times.

Fertilizer: None required while plants are in this arrangement.

COMMENTS: Since the cultural needs of the plants in this bowl garden are not entirely compatible, it is meant to be enjoyed for a few days or up to a week or two, more as a flower arrangement than as a permanent planting.

Growing arrangement in gardener's workbasket.

FIVE

Hiding pots with decorative containers that are waterproof

The bowl gardens in this chapter vary from almost instant to fairly ambitious combinations involving numerous plants. The easiest simply require slipping a pretty plant in a utilitarian pot into a cachepot, jardiniere or other decorative, waterproof container. Some are intended as more or less permanent plantings, others should be considered only as decorative arrangements for special occasions.

Dwarf orange or calamondin (*Citrofortunella mitis*) serves as a natu-
rally decorated tree centerpiece for a Christmas table. Created by
Bob Springman for Tiffany & Company. Photograph courtesy Tiffany
& Company.

61   Sedum in cachepot

CONTAINER: Glazed ceramic cachepot. *Sources:* Department stores, with china and glassware.

PLANT: *Sedum spectabile variegatum. Sources:* Nurseries, garden centers or by mail from specialists (see Appendix).

SPECIAL PLANTING TECHNIQUE: Place an inch-deep layer of pebbles or gravel in bottom, sprinkle with charcoal chips, then slip potted plant inside.

OWNER: James McNair.

ENVIRONMENT:

Light: Half day or more of sun.

Temperature: Cool to moderate (40–70° F.) in fall and winter, average dwelling or office in spring and summer.

Humidity: Low to medium, with fresh air.

Soil Mix: All-purpose (see Chapter One).

Soil Moisture: Evenly moist to on the dry side.

Fertilizer: Make light applications in spring and summer only.

COMMENTS: This sedum will survive winter cold to below zero when planted in the ground outdoors. However, as a container plant it is best wintered in a coldframe, pit greenhouse, cool sunny window or other protected place. Its leaves are yellow and bluish green; clusters of pink flowers appear in late summer, after which time the old stems should be cut back to make way for new growth, but not before the plant has been subjected to near-freezing temperatures for six to eight weeks.

Sedum in cachepot.

62   Natal-plum garden

CONTAINER: Glazed white ceramic cylinder. *Sources:* Plant shops or with china and glassware in department stores.

PLANT: Dwarf Natal-plum, a form of *Carissa. Sources:* Plant shops, nurseries or by mail from specialists (see Appendix).

SPECIAL PLANTING TECHNIQUE: Place an inch-deep layer of pebbles or gravel in bottom, sprinkle with charcoal chips, then slip potted plant inside.

OWNER: James McNair.

ENVIRONMENT:

Light: Half day or more of sun, or grow in a fluorescent-light garden.

Temperature: Moderate (55–70° F.) in fall and winter, average dwelling or office in spring and summer.

Humidity: Medium, with fresh-air circulation. Mist frequently.

Soil Mix: All-purpose (see Chapter One).

Soil Moisture: Evenly moist at all times.

Fertilizer: Make light applications in spring and summer only.

COMMENTS: This broadleaf tropical evergreen makes a superb subject for bonsai training. In season it has fragrant white flowers, followed by attractive fruit that turns red when ripe.

Natal-plum garden.

63   Tropical garden in roaster

CONTAINER: Enamelware turkey roaster. *Sources:* Supermarkets, dime, hardware and department stores.

PLANTS: Schefflera (for height) and hoya (for ground cover). *Sources:* Plant shops or by mail (see Appendix).

SPECIAL PLANTING TECHNIQUE: Place an inch-deep layer of pebbles or gravel in bottom, sprinkle with charcoal chips, then arrange individual potted plants inside. Carpet the surface with florist sheet moss to hide the pot rims.

OWNER: James McNair.

ENVIRONMENT:

Light: Half day or more of sun.

Temperature: Average dwelling or office.

Humidity: Medium, with fresh air. Mist frequently.

Soil Mix: All-purpose (see Chapter One).

Soil Moisture: Evenly moist to slightly on the dry side.

Fertilizer: Make light applications, mostly in spring and summer.

COMMENTS: For a sunny kitchen or breakfast-room window, try filling a roaster like this with individual pots of your favorite herbs.

Tropical garden in roaster.

64   **Walking iris in pre-Columbian head**

CONTAINER: One-of-a-kind pre-Columbian head. *Source:* Stendahl Galleries, Los Angeles.

PLANT: *Neomarica gracilis* (walking iris). *Sources:* Plant shops or by mail (see Appendix).

SPECIAL PLANTING TECHNIQUE: For a valuable piece of art like this I recommend coating the inside with petroleum jelly and lining with heavy-duty polyethylene plastic. Place an inch-deep layer of pebbles or gravel in bottom, sprinkle with charcoal chips, then slip potted plant inside.

OWNER: James McNair.

ENVIRONMENT:

Light: Half day or more of sun.

Temperature: Average dwelling or office.

Humidity: Medium, with fresh air.

Soil Mix: All-purpose (see Chapter One).

Soil Moisture: Evenly moist to slightly on the dry side.

Fertilizer: Make light applications in spring and summer.

COMMENTS: Walking iris makes a beautiful foliage plant in all seasons, but it also produces showy flowers from time to time.

Walking iris in pre-Columbian head.

65   Maidenhair fern in pre-Columbian bowl

CONTAINER: One-of-a-kind pre-Columbian bowl. *Source:* Stendahl Galleries, Los Angeles.

PLANT: *Adiantum* (maidenhair fern). *Sources:* Plant shops or by mail (see Appendix).

SPECIAL PLANTING TECHNIQUE: For a valuable piece of art like this I recommend coating the inside with petroleum jelly and lining with heavy-duty polyethylene plastic. Then place an inch-deep layer of pebbles or gravel in bottom, sprinkle with charcoal chips and slip potted plant inside. Carpet the soil surface with florist sheet moss or pebbles.

OWNER: James McNair.

ENVIRONMENT:

Light: Bright but little or no direct sun, or grow in a fluorescent-light garden.

Temperature: Average dwelling or office, preferably not over 70° F. during the winter heating season.

Humidity: Medium to high. Mist frequently.

Soil Mix: All-purpose (see Chapter One).

Soil Moisture: Evenly moist at all times.

Fertilizer: Make light applications occasionally all year.

COMMENTS: A planting like this shows off to best advantage when placed high enough to be seen in profile.

Maidenhair fern in pre-Columbian bowl.

66   Euonymus in mixing bowl

CONTAINER: French tin mixing bowl. *Sources:* With housewares in department stores or in gourmet cookware shops.

PLANT: *Euonymus Fortunei* 'Emerald Cushion.' *Sources:* Local nurseries or by mail from specialists (see Appendix).

SPECIAL PLANTING TECHNIQUE: To prevent rust, coat the inside with petroleum jelly and line with heavy-duty polyethylene plastic. Place an inch-deep layer of pebbles or gravel in bottom, sprinkle with charcoal chips and slip potted plant inside. Carpet the surface with florist sheet moss.

OWNER: James McNair.

ENVIRONMENT:

Light: Half day or more of sun, or grow in a fluorescent-light garden.

Temperature: Cool to moderate (35–65° F.) in fall and winter, average dwelling or office in spring and summer.

Humidity: Medium, with fresh air. Mist frequently.

Soil Mix: All-purpose (see Chapter One).

Soil Moisture: Evenly moist at all times.

Fertilizer: Make light applications in spring and summer.

COMMENTS:. Prune as necessary to maintain desired size and shape.

Euonymus in mixing bowl.

67   Bird's-nest fern in earthenware

CONTAINER: Contemporary Columbian pottery. *Sources:* Plant shops, department stores.

PLANT: *Asplenium nidus* (bird's-nest fern). *Sources:* Plant shops or by mail (see Appendix).

SPECIAL PLANTING TECHNIQUE: Place an inch-deep layer of pebbles or gravel in bottom, sprinkle with charcoal chips and slip potted plant inside.

OWNER: James McNair.

ENVIRONMENT:

Light: Bright, up to a half day of sun, or grow in a fluorescent-light garden.

Temperature: Average dwelling or office.

Humidity: Medium to high. Mist frequently.

Soil Mix: All-purpose (see Chapter One).

Soil Moisture: Evenly moist at all times.

Fertilizer: Make light applications in spring and summer.

COMMENTS: For maximum effect place on shelf or pedestal with back- or uplighting at night.

Bird's-nest fern in earthenware.

68   High-rise bowl garden

CONTAINERS: Stacked plastic bowls by Heller. *Sources:* Department stores.

PLANTS: Small plant of dwarf boxwood (*Buxus*) with ground cover of selaginella. *Sources:* Plant shops or by mail from specialists. Vial of water inserted in soil holds cut nasturtium flowers.

SPECIAL PLANTING TECHNIQUE: Coat the inside of the bowl with petroleum jelly and line with heavy-duty polyethylene plastic. Place a half-inch layer of pebbles in bottom, sprinkle with charcoal chips. Plant directly in the bowl. Carpet bare soil with pebbles or green woods moss. Add vial of fresh water and flowers for special occasions.

OWNER: James McNair.

ENVIRONMENT:

Light: Up to a half day of sun, or grow in a fluorescent-light garden.

Temperature: Moderate (55–70° F.) in fall and winter, average dwelling or office in spring and summer.

Humidity: Medium to high, with fresh-air circulation. Mist frequently.

Soil Mix: All-purpose (see Chapter One).

Soil Moisture: Evenly moist at all times.

Fertilizer: Make light applications in spring and summer.

COMMENTS: This bowl garden idea has endless variations, depending on the plant materials available.

High-rise bowl garden.

69   **Bonsai tray garden of tropicals**

CONTAINER: Glazed ceramic bonsai tray. *Sources:* Bonsai specialists, plant shops.

PLANTS: Dwarf gloxinia, episcia (flame violet), miniature rex begonia, upright cane begonia and a seedling of a tropical tree. *Sources:* Plant shops or by mail (see Appendix).

SPECIAL PLANTING TECHNIQUE: This bowl garden is quick to assemble and, since the plants are left in their individual pots, it is possible to remove one without disturbing the others. Position pots in the container until you achieve a pleasing effect. Fill in the spaces between the pots with moist sphagnum moss, hiding all the pots completely with additional layers of moss. A small rock completes the planting.

OWNERS: George and Virginie Elbert.

Bonsai tray garden of tropicals.

Blue delftware planter.

Silver bowl garden.

Growing arrangement in gardener's workbasket.

Washtub garden.

Fernery in a basket.

Shrimp plant creole.

Fish poacher window box.

Maidenhair fern
in pre-Columbian bowl.

Salad bowl garden.

Chicago plant shop owner Paul
Galka holds a polyscias bonsai;
a lipstick vine hangs behind him.

ENVIRONMENT:

> *Light:* Up to a half day of sun or grow in a fluorescent-light garden.
>
> *Temperature:* Average dwelling or office.
>
> *Humidity:* Medium to high. Mist frequently.
>
> *Soil Mix:* All-purpose (see Chapter One).
>
> *Soil Moisture:* Evenly moist at all times.
>
> *Fertilizer:* Make light applications all year.

COMMENTS: The technique used to create this tray garden may be used just as effectively for larger containers and plants of all sizes. For example, in my office I have a woven basket approximately 20 inches deep by 24 inches in diameter. After lining it with a double thickness of heavy-duty polyethylene plastic, I arranged inside each of the following plants, all in individual containers: five-foot kentia palm, five small- to medium-size bromeliads and two miniature philodendrons (one with burgundy leaves, the other with golden green). I used chunks of osmunda fiber to establish each pot at the desired level and then carpeted over all with florist sheet moss. This planting receives a half day of sun.

70   **Tropical garden in antique brass container**

CONTAINER: Antique brass. *Sources:* Antique dealers, junk shops, with fireplace equipment in department stores.

PLANTS: English ivy, fittonia, peperomia, ferns, rhizomatous begonia, African violet. *Sources:* Plant shops or by mail (see Appendix).

SPECIAL PLANTING TECHNIQUE: Coat the inside with petroleum jelly and line with heavy-duty polyethylene plastic. Place an inch-deep layer of pebbles in bottom and sprinkle with charcoal chips. Add plants in their individual containers. Hide pots with florist sheet moss.

OWNER: Longwood Gardens, Kennett Square, Pennsylvania.

ENVIRONMENT:

Light: Up to a half day of sun, or grow in a fluorescent-light garden.

Temperature: Average dwelling or office.

Humidity: Medium to high. Mist frequently.

Soil Mix: All-purpose (see Chapter One).

Soil Moisture: Evenly moist at all times.

Fertilizer: Make light applications all year.

COMMENTS: The chief key to success with mixed plantings like this is to combine only plants that are culturally compatible. Promptly remove withered flowers and dead leaves.

Tropical garden in antique brass container.

71   Bowl of growing exotica

CONTAINER: Glazed ceramic bowl. *Sources:* Plant shops, department stores, garden centers.

PLANTS: Rhizomatous begonia, dwarf peperomia, silver-and-green *Dracaena goldieana*. *Sources:* Plant shops or by mail (see Appendix).

SPECIAL PLANTING TECHNIQUE: Place an inch-deep layer of pebbles in the bottom and sprinkle with charcoal chips. Arrange potted plants inside or remove pots and plant directly in the bowl.

OWNER: Longwood Gardens, Kennett Square, Pennsylvania.

ENVIRONMENT:

Light: Up to a half day of sun.

Temperature: Average dwelling or office.

Humidity: Medium. Mist frequently.

Soil Mix: All-purpose (see Chapter One).

Soil Moisture: Evenly moist at all times.

Fertilizer: Make light applications in spring and summer.

COMMENTS: Although any plants that are culturally compatible may be grouped in the same container, for maximum effect choose contrasting colors, shapes and textures.

Bowl of growing exotica.

72   Holiday centerpiece garden

CONTAINER: Silver bowl. *Sources:* Tiffany's provided the one shown; also other jewelers or with silver in department stores.

PLANTS: Amaryllis surrounded by red-flowering dwarf hybrids of *Kalanchoe Blossfeldiana. Sources:* Plant shops at Christmas time.

SPECIAL PLANTING TECHNIQUE: Coat the inside of the bowl with petroleum jelly and line with heavy-duty polyethylene plastic. Place an inch-deep layer of pebbles in the bottom and sprinkle with charcoal chips. Arrange potted plants inside and carpet the surface with florist sheet moss or remove plants from pots and place directly in the bowl.

OWNER: Created by Bob Springman for Tiffany.

ENVIRONMENT:

Light: Half day or more of sun.

Temperature: Average dwelling or office.

Humidity: Medium.

Soil Mix: All-purpose (see Chapter One).

Soil Moisture: Keep kalanchoe evenly moist to on the dry side. Keep amaryllis moist except dry in early fall while the bulb is resting.

Fertilizer: Make light applications in spring and summer.

COMMENTS: While amaryllis makes an excellent house plant, I find kalanchoes of this type difficult to rebloom since they require short days and long nights in autumn in order to initiate budding. I recommend treating this bowl garden as a long-lasting flower arrangement and not as a permanent planting. Once plants like this are in bloom, too much hot, direct sun shortens their life, while strong natural light encourages good color and maximum life.

Holiday centerpiece garden.

73   Hibachi garden

CONTAINER: Cast-iron hibachi. *Sources:* Department and hardware stores.

PLANTS: Angel-wing and cane begonias, fittonia, English ivy and episcia (flame violet). *Sources:* Plant shops or by mail (see Appendix).

SPECIAL PLANTING TECHNIQUE: To prevent rust, coat the inside with petroleum jelly and line with heavy-duty polyethylene plastic. Place an inch-deep layer of pebbles or gravel in the bottom, sprinkle with charcoal chips and slip potted plants inside. Carpet the surface with florist sheet moss.

OWNER: Longwood Gardens, Kennett Square, Pennsylvania.

ENVIRONMENT:

Light: Up to a half day of sun, or grow in a fluorescent-light garden.

Temperature: Average dwelling or office.

Humidity: Medium to high. Mist frequently.

Soil Mix: All-purpose (see Chapter One).

Soil Moisture: Evenly moist at all times.

Fertilizer: Make light applications all year.

COMMENTS: Since the plants in this bowl garden remain in their own pots, it is easy to remove one without disturbing the others. Take care, however, not to water so much at any given time that the bases of the pots are left standing in the excess drainage. Success with a mixed planting like this depends partly on catering to the individual moisture needs of each plant, and since separate containers are used, this is easy to do; just turn back the moss and pinch a little of the surface soil in every pot before applying water.

Hibachi garden.

74   Fish poacher window box

CONTAINER: Aluminum fish poacher. *Sources:* Department stores and gourmet cookware shops.

PLANTS: Tree and trailing lantanas, dwarf nandina bushes and English ivy. *Sources:* Plant shops, nurseries or by mail (see Appendix).

SPECIAL PLANTING TECHNIQUE: Coat inside of the container with petroleum jelly, then line with heavy-duty polyethylene plastic. Add a layer of drainage pebbles in the bottom if you want to plant directly in it, otherwise simply arrange potted plants inside. Carpet the surface with florist sheet moss.

OWNER: James McNair.

ENVIRONMENT:

Light: Half day or more of sun.

Temperature: Cool to moderate (50–70° F.) in fall and winter, average dwelling or office in spring and summer.

Humidity: Medium to high with fresh-air circulation. Mist frequently.

Soil Mix: All-purpose (see Chapter One).

Soil Moisture: Evenly moist at all times.

COMMENTS: A fish poacher like this makes an especially nice container for a kitchen window garden.

Fish poacher window box.

Appendixes

A small saintpaulia (left) and pilea planted in shells.

Appendix: Ready-reference lists of plant materials for bowl garden landscapes

(Note: The abbreviation "fl." following a plant indicates that it is cultivated for flowers in season)

GROUND COVERS, VINES, TRAILERS

Miniature (about 1 inch tall)
Ficus pumila (creeping fig)
Selaginella species and varieties
Soleirolia Soleirolii (baby's-tears)

Dwarf (about 3 to 6 inches tall)
Allophyton mexicanum (Mexican foxglove) fl.
Callisia species
Chamaeranthemum species
Cryptanthus species (earth-star bromeliads)
Cyanotis species
Cymbalaria muralis (Kenilworth ivy)
Episcia species and varieties; fl.
Fittonia species (nerve plant)
Glechoma hederacea variegata
Hedera helix varieties (English ivy)
Hoya species and varieties (wax plant); fl.
Lamium Galeobdolon variegatum
Maranta species and varieties (prayer plant)
Pellionia species
Peperomia, trailing species
Pilea species
Plectranthus species
Saxifraga stolonifera (strawberry-geranium; strawberry-begonia)
Sedum species and varieties
Sempervivum species and varieties
Tradescantia species and varieties (wandering Jew)
Zebrina species and varieties (wandering Jew)

GRASS OR GRASSLIKE

Miniature (to about 3 inches tall)
Acorus gramineus pusillus

Dwarf (to about 6 inches tall)
Acorus gramineus variegatus
Bambusa, dwarf species (bamboo)
Chlorophytum Bichetii (dwarf spider plant)
Liriope Muscari variegata (to 16 inches)
Ophiopogon japonicus (dwarf lilyturf)
Stenotaphrum secundatum variegatum (variegated St. Augustine grass)

SHRUB OR SHRUBLIKE FORM

Miniature, to 12 inches
(* - as bonsai subjects)
* *Buxus microphylla japonica* (Japanese littleleaf boxwood)
* *Calliandra* species; fl.
* *Carissa* species and varieties; fl.
Cissus striata (dwarf grape-ivy)
Crossandra infundibuliformis; fl.
* *Daphne odora;* fl.
* *Deutzia gracilis;* fl.
Euonymus japonica microphylla variegatus
Malpighia coccigera; fl.
Myrtus communis (myrtle)
* *Pelargonium* species and varieties (geranium, especially miniature and dwarf cultivars)
* *Rosmarinus officinalis* (rosemary)
Teucrium species (germander)

To 3 feet tall
Abutilon (flowering maple); fl.
Allamanda; fl.
Aloysia triphylla (lemon-verbena)
Ardisia crispa (coral berry); fl.
Bauhinia variegata; fl.
Carissa species and varieties; fl.
Cestrum nocturnum; fl.

Citrus; fl. and fruit
Clerodendrum; fl.
Cuphea hyssopifolia; fl.
Daphne odora; fl.
Deutzia gracilis; fl.
Eranthemum nervosum; fl.
Fuchsia; fl.
Gardenia; fl.
Ixora; fl.
Jasminum (jasmine); fl.
Justicia Brandegeana (shrimp plant); fl.
Lantana; fl.
Medinilla magnifica; fl.
Nicodemia diversifolia (indoor oak)
Osmanthus fragrans (sweet-olive); fl.
Plumbago capensis; fl.
Serissa foetida variegata
Tibouchina semidecandra (glory-bush); fl.

TREE OR TREELIKE FORM

Miniature, to 18 inches
   (* - as bonsai subjects)
   Aeonium arboreum atropurpureum
 * *Aloysia triphylla* (lemon-verbena)
 * *Araucaria heterophylla* (Norfolk Island pine)
 * *Ardisia crispa* (coral berry); fl.
 * *Beaucarnea recurvata* (ponytail)
 * *Begonia* species and varieties (semituberous types); fl.
   Biophytum zenkeri
 * *Bougainvillea;* fl.
 * *Brunfelsia* species; fl.
 * *Calliandra* species; fl.
 * *Camellia;* fl.
 * *Citrus;* fl. and fruit
 * *Coffea arabica* (coffee tree)
 * *Eugenia*
   Euphorbia Milii (crown of thorns); fl.
 * *Ficus benjamina* (weeping fig)
 * *Gardenia;* fl.

* *Grevillea*
* *Ixora;* fl.
* *Jacaranda*
* *Jasminum* (jasmine); fl.
* *Laurus nobilis* (sweet bay)
* *Myrtus communis* (myrtle)
* *Nicodemia diversifolia* (indoor oak)
* *Olea europaea* (olive)
* *Osmanthus fragrans* (sweet-olive); fl.
* *Pelargonium* species and varieties (miniature and dwarf geraniums); fl.
* *Poinciana pulcherrima;* fl.
Polyscias fruticosa (ming aralia)
Portulacaria afra variegata (elephant bush)
Punica Granatum Nana (dwarf pomegranate); fl.
* *Pyracantha coccinea* cultivars (firethorn); fl. and berries
* *Rosmarinus officinalis* (rosemary)
* *Serissa foetida variegata*

To 8 feet (or more)

Abutilon (flowering maple); fl.
Aloysia triphylla (lemon-verbena)
Alsophila (tree-fern)
Araucaria heterophylla (Norfolk Island pine)
Ardisia crispa (coral berry); fl. and berries
Bauhinia variegata; fl.
Beaucarnea recurvata (ponytail)
Brunfelsia species; fl.
Camellia; fl.
Citrus; fl. and fruit
Coffea (coffee)
Dizygotheca
Eugenia
Euphorbia trigona
Ficus benjamina (weeping fig)
Grevillea
Hibiscus Rosa-sinensis (Chinese hibiscus); fl.
Lantana; fl.
Laurus nobilis (sweet bay)
Musa species (banana); fl.
Nerium Oleander; fl.
Olea europaea (olive)
Osmanthus fragrans; fl.

Persea americana (avocado)
Pleomele reflexa
Poinciana pulcherrima; fl.
Polyscias species and varieties
Sparmannia africana (indoor linden)
Tibouchina semidecandra (glory-bush); fl.
Trevesia palmata Sanderi (snowflake plant)

This giant bowl garden in entry area features a dwarfed pine tree
and the succulent, bright green rosettes of *aeoniums.* This container
has drainage holes; see Chapter Two. Photograph by Max Tatch.

Appendix: Plants and supplies by mail

Abbey Garden, 176 Toro Canyon Road, Carpinteria, California 93013. Complete listing of cacti and other succulents; 50¢ for catalog.

Abbot's Nursery, Route 4, Box 482, Mobile, Alabama 36609. Camellias.

Alberts & Merkel Brothers, Inc., 2210 South Federal Highway, Boynton Beach, Florida 33435. Orchids, plus an amazing array of tropical foliage and flowering house plants; 75¢ for list.

Alpenglow Gardens, 13328 King George Highway, Surrey, British Columbia V3T2T6, Canada. Hardy alpines and shrubs; $1. for catalog.

Antonelli Brothers, 2545 Capitola Road, Santa Cruz, California 95060. Tuberous begonias, gloxinias, achimenes.

Louise Barnaby, 12178 Highview Street, Vicksburg, Michigan 49097. African violets; send stamp for list.

Mrs. Mary V. Boose, 9 Turney Place, Trumbull, Connecticut 06611. African violets and episcias; 25¢ for list.

John Brudy's Rare Plant House, P. O. Box 1348, Cocoa Beach, Florida 32931. Unusual seeds and plants; $1. for catalog.

Buell's Greenhouses, Weeks Road, Eastford, Connecticut 06242. Complete listing of gloxinias, African violets and other gesneriads; $1. for catalog.

Burgess Seed & Plant Company, 67 East Battle Creek, Galesburg, Michigan 49053. House plants, bulbs, nursery stock.

Henry Field Seed and Nursery Company, 407 Sycamore, Shenandoah, Iowa 51601. House plants, nursery stock, supplies.

Fernwood Plants, 1311 Fernwood Pacific Drive, Topanga, California 90290. Rare and unusual cacti; 50¢ for catalog.

Fischer Greenhouses, Linwood, New Jersey 08221. African violets and and other gesneriads; supplies; 25¢ for catalog.

Floralite Company, 2124 East Oakwood Road, Oak Creek, Wisconsin 53154. Fluorescent-light gardening equipment and supplies.

Fox Orchids, 6615 West Markham, Little Rock, Arkansas 72205. Orchids and supplies for growing them at home.

Arthur Freed Orchids, Inc., 5731 South Bonsall Drive, Malibu, California 90265. Orchids and supplies for growing them at home.

J. Howard French, P. O. Box 87, Center Rutland, Vermont 05736. Bulbs.

Girard Nurseries, P. O. Box 428, Geneva, Ohio 44041. Bonsai supplies.

Golden Plant Nurseries, Inc., 7300 Astro Street, Orlando, Florida 32807. Rare flowering gingers, new hybrid spathiphyllums, other exotics; 50¢ for list.

Grigsby Cactus Gardens, 2354 Bella Vista Drive, Vista, California 92083. Cacti and other succulents; 50¢ for catalog.

Gurney Seed and Nursery Company, Yankton, South Dakota 57078. Seeds, bulbs, plants.

Orchids by Hausermann, Inc., P. O. Box 363, Elmhurst, Illinois 60126. Orchids; supplies; $1.25 for catalog.

W. Atlee Burpee Company, Warminster, Pennsylvania 18974. Seeds, bulbs, supplies and equipment; home greenhouses.

David Buttram, P. O. Box 193, Independence, Missouri 64051. African violets; 25¢ for list.

Cactus Gem Nursery, 10092 Mann Drive, Cupertino, California (visit Thursday–Sunday); by mail write P. O. Box 327, Aromas, California 95004.

Castle Violets, 614 Castle Road, Colorado Springs, Colorado 80904. African violets.

Champion's African Violets, 8848 Van Hoesen Road, Clay, New York 13041. African violets; send stamp for list.

Victor Constaninov, 3321 21st Street, Apartment 7, San Francisco, California 94110. African violets, other gesneriads; send stamp for list.

Cook's Geranium Nursery, 714 North Grand, Lyons, Kansas 67544. Geraniums; 50¢ for catalog.

P. de Jager and Sons, 188 Asbury Street, South Hamilton, Massachusetts 01982. Bulbs for forcing as well as all other types for indoors/outdoors.

Electric Farm, 104 B Lee Road, Oak Hill, New York 12460. Gesneriads; send self-addressed stamped envelope for list.

Farmer Seed and Nursery Company, Inc., Faribault, Minnesota 55021. House plants, nursery stock.

Sim T. Holmes, 100 Tustarawas Road, Beaver, Pennsylvania 15009. African violets, miniature and regular.

Spencer M. Howard Orchid Imports, 11802 Huston Street, North Hollywood, California 91607. Unusual orchids.

Gordon M. Hoyt Orchids, Seattle Heights, Washington 98036. Orchids; supplies.

Margaret Ilgenfritz Orchids, Blossom Lane, P. O. Box 665, Monroe, Michigan. Orchids; supplies; $1. for catalog.

Jones and Scully, 2200 North West 33rd Avenue, Miami, Florida 33142. Orchids and supplies: $3.50 for color catalog.

Kartuz Greenhouses, 92 Chestnut Street, Wilmington, Massachusetts 01887. Gesneriads, begonias, house plants in general; supplies; 50¢ for catalog.

Kirkpatrick's, 27785 de Anza Street, Barstow, California 92311. Cacti and other succulents; 25¢ for list.

K & L Cactus Nursery, 12712 Stockton Boulevard, Galt, California 95632. Complete selection of cacti and other succulents; list 50¢.

Lauray, Undermountain Road, Route 41, Salisbury, Connecticut 06068. Gesneriads, cacti and other succulents, begonias; 50¢ for catalog.

Logee's Greenhouses, 55 North Street, Danielson, Connecticut 06239. Complete selection of house plants, with special emphasis on begonias, geraniums, plus herbs; $1. for catalog.

Loyce's Flowers, Route 2, Box 11, Granbury, Texas 76048. Specialist in hoyas; also bougainvillea and hibiscus; 50¢ for list.

Lyndon Lyon, 14 Mutchler Street, Dolgeville, New York 13329. African violets and other gesneriads; miniature roses.

Rod McLellan Company, 1450 El Camino Real, South San Francisco, California 94080. Orchids; supplies.

Earl May Seed and Nursery Company, Shenandoah, Iowa 51603. Seeds, bulbs, plants.

Merry Gardens, Camden, Maine 04843. House plants and herbs; large selection of begonias and geraniums; $1. for catalog.

Mini-Roses, P. O. Box 245, Station A, Dallas, Texas 75208. Miniature roses.

Modlin's Cactus Gardens, Route 4, Box 3034, Vista, California 92083. Cacti and other succulents; 25¢ for catalog.

Cactus by Mueller, 10411 Rosedale Highway, Bakersfield, California 93308. Cacti and other succulents; 25¢ for list.

Walter F. Nicke, P. O. Box 667, Hudson, New York 12534; 25¢ for catalog of supplies and tools for gardening, many from Europe.

Nuccio's Nurseries, 3555 Chaney Trail, Altadena, California 91001. Hybrid camellias and azaleas.

Orinda Nursery, Bridgeville, Delaware 19933. Hybrid camellias.

George W. Park Seed Company, Inc., Greenwood, South Carolina 29647. Seeds, bulbs, plants, supplies.

John Scheepers, Inc., 63 Wall Street, New York, New York 10005. Flowering bulbs.

Sequoia Nursery, 2519 East Noble Street, Visalia, California 93277. Miniature roses.

Shaffer's Tropical Gardens, Inc., 3220 41 Avenue, Capitola, California 95010. Orchids.

Singers' Growing Things, 6385 Enfield Avenue, Reseda, California 91335. Cacti and other succulents; 50¢ for list.

Smith's Cactus Garden, P. O. Box 871, Paramount, California 90723. Cacti and other succulents; 50¢ for catalog.

Fred A. Stewart, Inc., Orchids, 1212 East Las Tunas Drive, San Gabriel, California 91778. Orchids; supplies.

Ed Storms, 4223 Pershing, Fort Worth, Texas 76107. Lithops and other succulents; 50¢ for catalog.

Sunnybrook Farms, 9448 Mayfield Road, Chesterland, Ohio 44026. Herbs, scented geraniums, house plants, sedums and sempervivums; 50¢ for catalog.

Sunnyslope Gardens, 8638 Huntington Drive, San Gabriel, California 91775. Chrysanthemums; supplies.

Thon's Garden Mums, 4815 Oak Street, Crystal Lake, Illinois 60014. Chrysanthemums.

Tinari Greenhouses, Box 190, 2325 Valley Road, Huntingdon Valley, Pennsylvania 19006. African violets, gesneriads; supplies; 25¢ for catalog.

Wayside Gardens, Hodges, South Carolina 29695. Color catalog of nursery stock; supplies; containers; $1. for catalog.

White Flower Farm, Litchfield, Connecticut 06759. Spectacular English hybrid plants and bulbs; imported containers; supplies; $3.50 for catalog, itself a work of art.

Wilson Brothers, Roachdale, Indiana 47121. House plants, with special emphasis on geraniums.

Appendix: Specialized plant societies and periodicals

African Violet Magazine, bi-monthly publication of the African Violet Society of America, Inc., Box 1326, Knoxville, Tennessee 37901.

American Fern Journal, quarterly publication of the American Fern Society, Biological Sciences Group, University of Connecticut, Storrs, Connecticut 06268.

American Orchid Society Bulletin, monthly publication of the American Orchid Society, Inc., Botanical Museum of Harvard University, Cambridge, Massachusetts 02138.

The Begonia, monthly of the American Begonia Society, Inc., 139 North Ledoux Road, Beverly Hills, California 90211.

Bonsai (quarterly) and *ABStracts* (monthly newsletter), publications of the American Bonsai Society, 953 South Shore Drive, Lake Waukomis, Parksville, Missouri 64151.

Bonsai Magazine, ten-times-a-year publication of Bonsai Clubs International, 445 Blake Street, Menlo Park, California 94025.

The Bromeliad Journal, bi-monthly publication of the Bromeliad Society, Inc., P. O. Box 3279, Santa Monica, California 90403.

Cactus and Succulent Journal, bi-monthly publication of the Cactus and Succulent Society of America, Inc., Box 167, Reseda, California 91335.

The Camellia Journal, quarterly publication of the American Camellia Society, Box 212, Fort Valley, Georgia 31030.

Cymbidium Society News, monthly publication of the Cymbidium Society of America, Inc., 6787 Worsham Drive, Whittier, California 90602.

Epiphyllum Bulletin, publication of the Epiphyllum Society of America, 218 East Greystone Avenue, Monrovia, California 91016.

Geraniums Around the World, quarterly publication of the International Geranium Society, 11960 Pascal Avenue, Colton, California 92324.

Gesneriad Saintpaulia News, bi-monthly publication of the American Gesneriad Society, 11983 Darlington Avenue, Los Angeles, California 99049.

The Gloxinian, bi-monthly publication of the American Gloxinia and Gesneriad Society, Inc., P. O. Box 174, New Milford, Connecticut 06776.

Hobby Greenhouse Owners' Association of America, Box 674, Corte Madera, California 94925.

House Plants and Porch Gardens, monthly magazine, Deacon's Way, New Canaan, Connecticut 06840.

Light Garden, bi-monthly publication of the Indoor Light Gardening Society of America, Inc., 128 West 58th Street, New York, New York 10019.

Monthly Fern Lessons, with newsletter and annual magazine, publications of the Los Angeles International Fern Society, 2423 Burritt Avenue, Redondo Beach, California 90278.

The National Fuchsia Fan, monthly publication of the National Fuchsia Society, 10934 East Flory Street, Whittier, California 90606.

The Orchid Digest, 25 Ash Avenue, Corte Madera, California 94925.

Plantlife-Amaryllis Yearbook, bulletin of the American Plant Life Society, Box 150, La Jolla, California 92037.

Plants Alive, monthly magazine about indoor gardening, 1255 Portland Place, Boulder, Colorado 80302.

Popular Gardening Indoors, bi-monthly magazine about indoor gardening, 383 Madison Avenue, New York, New York 10017.

Princepes, quarterly publication of the Palm Society, 1320 South Venetian Way, Miami, Florida 33139.

Seed Pod, quarterly publication of the American Hibiscus Society, Box 98, Eagle Lake, Florida 33139.

Terrarium Topics, published by the Terrarium Association, 57 Wolfpit Avenue, Norwalk, Connecticut 06851.

Under Glass, bi-monthly devoted to home greenhouse growing, Irvington, New York 10533.

Bibliography

Ballard, Ernesta Drinker. *The Art of Training Plants.* New York: Harper & Row, Publishers, Inc., 1962; Barnes & Noble, 1974.

————. *Growing Plants Indoors.* New York: Barnes & Noble, 1971; published originally as *Garden in Your House.* New York: Harper & Row, Publishers, Inc., 1958.

Elbert, George A. and Virginie F. *The Miracle Houseplants: The Gesneriads.* New York: Crown Publishers, Inc., 1976.

Fitch, Charles Marden. *The Complete Book of Houseplants Under Lights.* New York: Hawthorn Books, Inc., 1975.

————. *The Complete Book of Miniature Roses.* New York: Hawthorn Books, Inc., 1977.

Graf, Albert B. *Exotic Plant Manual.* Rutherford, New Jersey: Julius Roehrs Co., 1970.

Howarth, Sheila. *Miniature Gardens.* New York: Arco Publishing Co., Inc., 1977.

Kramer, Jack. *Miniature Gardens in Bowl, Dish and Tray.* New York: Charles Scribner's Sons, 1975.

McDonald, Elvin. *Gardening in Containers.* New York: Grosset & Dunlap, 1975.

————. *House Plants Indoors/Outdoors.* San Francisco: Ortho Books, 1974.

————. *Little Plants for Small Spaces.* New York: Popular Library, 1974; M. Evans and Company, 1975.

————. *Plants as Therapy.* New York: Praeger Publishers, 1976; Popular Library, 1977.

————. *Stop Talking to Your Plants and Listen.* New York: Funk & Wagnalls, 1977.

———. *The World Book of House Plants.* New York: Funk & Wagnalls, 1975; Popular Library, 1976.

Yang, Linda. *The Terrace Gardener's Handbook.* New York: Doubleday & Company, Inc., 1975.

This high-rise bowl garden is based on a series of stacked clay pots, saucers and drain tiles. Flowering wax begonias, Iceland poppies and fairy primroses grow in individual pots that facilitate quick removal and replacement of anything past its prime. Photographed by the author in sunny plant room of Cleveland florist D. K. Vanderbrook.